D0851327

The
Small
Group
Trainer's
Survival
Guide

The Small Group Trainer's Survival Guide

Birge D. Reichard
Christiane M. F. Siewers
Paul Rodenhauser

SAGE Publications
International Educational and Professional Publisher
Newbury Park   London   New Delhi

For information address:

 SAGE Publications, Inc.
2455 Teller Road
Newbury Park, California 91320

SAGE Publications Ltd.
6 Bonhill Street
London EC2A 4PU
United Kingdom

SAGE Publications India Pvt. Ltd.
M-32 Market
Greater Kailash I
New Delhi 110 048 India

Printed in the United States of America

Library of Congress Cataloging-in-Publication Data

Reichard, Birge D.
    The small group trainer's survival guide / Birge D. Reichard,
Christiane M. F. Siewers, Paul Rodenhauser.
      p. cm.
    Includes bibliographical references and index.
    ISBN 0-8039-4740-2 (cl).—ISBN 0-8039-4757-7 (pb)
    1. Group relations training. 2. Psychic trauma—Prevention.
I. Siewers, Christiane M. F. II. Rodenhauser. Paul. III. Title.
HM134.R45   1992
158'.2—dc20   92-12442

93 94 95 10 9 8 7 6 5 4 3 2

Sage Production Editor: Astrid Virding

CONTENTS

PREFACE

This book is a product of joint authorship. As members of the Clinical Consultants' Committee of the National Training Laboratories (NTL) for more than ten years, the authors have a common interest in laboratory education, a term adopted by some behavioral scientists. We have, collectively, both organizational and clinical backgrounds and experience. All of us have experience as trainers and managers. Our training ranges from psychology and organization behavior to psychiatry. As colleagues, we have collaborated in a variety of ways to conduct or support a number of laboratory education events.

Although we share many views, we sometimes differ. One example is our difference about what constitutes stress of clinical proportion. Is it the point at which a participant reports a subjective experience and/or exhibits a noticeable behavioral reaction, or the point at which he or she can no longer participate in a laboratory education program? Does the question rest with the subjective, albeit professional, judgment of the group leader (trainer) or with the psychiatric consultant, or is it a more complex process demanding attention from everyone involved?

There is the question of risk in laboratory education. We will probably never be able to find a valid figure about the casualty rate from affective education. Not all programs declare that emotional learning is part of the educational method, not all cases of distress are known or reported and postevent difficulties of participants is largely unknown. In our own experience, the reported incidence of emotional distress is 1%. The same estimates were made by Seashore (1968) almost twenty-five years ago. Even if one assumes a larger number of casualties, one must ask if such a risk is any higher than the true casualty rate of daily organizational and personal stress. It is apparent, and with forethought, that we have included no specific differences in stress responses or appropriate interventions, between men and women, whites and people of color, and people of different cultures and people in different life stages. This work addresses issues and concerns the authors consider generic to the human race and characteristic of the human condition. This is an open book with chapters yet to be written as our knowledge of clinical disruptions in laboratory education increases.

This work was originally conceived as a tool for professional members of the NTL Institute for Applied Behavioral Science, which conducts numerous T-groups, or sensitivity training programs, as well as a variety of management and organizational programs that go beyond cognitive learning. As we progressed with the writing it became evident that the material might be useful to a wider audience, people who conduct experiential learning programs in the corporate world, religious organizations, government, educational systems, and so forth. In that so little has been written about distress management, we hope the work is helpful to this wider audience, even though the book contains some behavioral science buzz words like T-groups, which are the most popular, though not the only, form of what we term laboratory education.

Depending upon one's skills and knowledge in laboratory education, this book can be a reference, a refresher, an instructional aid, a frame of reference, or a conceptualizing aid. Hopefully, it will stimulate further reading, writing, and discussion. It might also aid in examining or establishing guidelines for laboratory training and laboratory trainers in particular settings or organizations. Again, though this is not a recipe for conducting laboratory education groups, we trust that it will be useful.

A colleague on the Clinical Consultants' Committee, Dr. Richard Lippincott, was an early contributor to this effort and deserves special recognition from the authors. Marilyn Swenson, a former executive on the central staff of NTL, also deserves special recognition. She contributed to the substance of this work as well as provided coordinating and administrative support. Without her work and encouragement, this book would still be "a nice project to do someday when we have the time!" Skye K. M. Rodenhauser edited the work.

1. WHAT IS LABORATORY EDUCATION?

In the behavioral sciences, *laboratory education* is a term used for learning events that go beyond the traditional classroom didactic method intended to evoke thoughts. The laboratory method utilizes experiential activities that, in addition to cognitive or intellectual material, evoke feelings which are then explored as part of the learning. The use of the word *laboratory* connotes the spirit of inquiry as participants are both the objects of study *and* the researchers. In laboratory education, participants experiment with and analyze their behavior, and they seek increased knowledge of self. Though there are no test tubes or Bunsen burners, it is a laboratory in the true sense of being a workplace for study and analysis.

The training group (T-group), also known as sensitivity training, is the prototype of the laboratory method of learning. This educational method was used more in earlier years for learning about group dynamics (Benne, Bradford, Gibb, & Lippitt, 1975). It underlies other small group approaches such as Gestalt programs, Tavistock conferences, encounter groups, marriage encounters, and so forth. As an educational method, it is also an underpinning of organizational consulting known variously as organization development (OD), organization effectiveness (OE), or

1

organization renewal (OR)—not to be confused with operations research—in which an action-research approach is used. The laboratory method has now been adapted to almost every setting in which education or training is conducted.

Salespeople role-play a cold call, then discuss the anxiety generated and their feelings of rejection when the sale is not made; counselors and psychotherapists pursue self-awareness training to better identify their biases or personal issues, which should not be inflicted upon clients or patients; executives examine their leadership styles in order to understand ways in which they manage conflict or deliver performance appraisals, and so on. Techniques such as role playing, small group discussion, personality inventories, one way-two way communications exercises, and psychodrama are some examples of activities that today are, in one form or another, commonly applied in all occupational settings.

Furthermore, in the context of the behavioral sciences, laboratory education is known by many names, such as T-group, sensitivity training, affective education, emancipatory education, human relations training, experiential learning, and andrological learning, to name but a few. Those who conduct these kinds of activities are known variously as trainers, facilitators, group consultants, group leaders, and even teachers. These people use a combination of experiential and affective learning in programs to increase self-awareness, improve interpersonal competence, encourage risk taking, build more cohesive groups or work teams, raise self esteem, and study group and organizational dynamics.

So you can see that what began as an educational method more than forty years ago with the birth of the T-group is now a part of most people's learning experience. Though this book was written originally for T-groups, or more emotionally intense learning events, it has relevance for everyone who engages in learning events in which there is a mix of feelings, thoughts, values, and behavior. More than likely it is the mix of these components that varies according to the specific program (Benne et al., 1975).

In any learning setting in which participants are asked to risk self-disclosure, consider feelings as well as thoughts and behavior, act without familiar roles, and live in temporary social systems in which the culture is considerably "different," they will likely experience stress. Studies of college students serve as an example (Moos & Van Dort, 1979; Walsh,

1975). Certainly T-groups are not the only settings in which psychological stress occurs. Generally speaking, the more intense the emotional component of the learning activity, the more relevant and useful this book should be. Laboratory training can and should be stressful, in the sense that positive stress results in growth and desired change (Selye, 1974). Some training designs and techniques, however, may inadvertently result in negative outcomes or distress, and it is the prevention and management of this state that is the purpose of this book. It is assumed that all practitioners of the laboratory method, by whatever label, have professional and ethical responsibilities for working toward maximum competence in balancing the learning with the risk of distress.

Evolution of Behavior-Related Laboratory Education

In the summer of 1946, a workshop on intergroup relations was held at the State Teachers College in New Britain, Connecticut, in order to better understand race relations. It was there that the laboratory method of learning about behavior was discovered. At the end of each day, the staff gathered to share observations. Participants learned about these sessions and began to participate. Observations by staff about individual and group behavior during the day stimulated more interest than did the day's program sessions. In addition, more learning seemed to occur from the feedback and analysis of such behavior than took place from the usual didactic and discussion methods used during the day. The accidental discovery of a behavior-related laboratory method—learning by doing, by analyzing, and by receiving feedback—had happened.

The primary leaders of that landmark 1946 workshop in Connecticut had specialized backgrounds in social psychology (Kurt Lewin and Ronald Lippitt), educational psychology (Leland Bradford), and the discipline from which psychology evolved—philosophy (Kenneth Benne). Lewin died in early 1947. Subsequently, Bradford, Benne, and Lippitt founded the National Training Laboratory in Group Development (NTL), which held its first residential laboratory in the summer of 1947 in Bethel, Maine. It is important to note that while these "founding fathers" of behavioral education in a laboratory setting had different special interests, they shared a solid grounding in the science of human behavior. The major body of group leaders who followed, such as the early NTL professional network, those at the Research Center for Group Dynamics at MIT, and at the Human Relations Center at Boston University were also highly trained behavioral scientists, though they had interdisciplinary interests. Surely they were influenced by psychoanalytic and other personality theories which were so prevalent during the 1940s and 1950s.

Psychiatry was also an important influence upon these laboratory methods and concepts. From the work of Wilfred Bion (1961) and his associates at the Tavistock Clinic in group methods of treating combat fatigue patients, to the "humanistic psychiatry" of Harry Stack Sullivan, and others who heightened interest in the study of interpersonal relations, this new form of laboratory education benefited from psychiatry. Indeed, a number of those early NTL network members were psychiatrists.

A significant modification to the original laboratory experience was the gradual but sure departure from Kurt Lewin's group and larger system orientation, toward an interpersonal and intrapersonal focus. This led to a more individual and psychological emphasis, as compared to sociological or social psychological emphasis, not only for programs but also for participants (Gottschalk & Pattison, 1969).

The evolution of the laboratory method related to human behavior inevitably led to some lack of clarity about the distinctions between laboratory learning and psychotherapy (Gottschalk & Pattison, 1969). The two fields are a fine example of paradox. That is, they are separate yet related. The discussion in this book will focus on their separateness. Both psychotherapy groups and T-groups, for example, focus on intrapersonal material and deal with learning or cognitive change. Therapy groups, in addition, intend to deal with psychological change or an alteration of personality structure. Both kinds of groups work on both kinds of change to some degree, but usually an implicit or explicit priority is given to one at the expense of the other, and the contract between trainers and participants is specified accordingly.

A classic article on the subject by Singer, Astrachan, Gould, and Klein (1975) describes the kinds of groups, their goals, issues, leader behaviors, and the overlap between the types of groups. Some groups focus more on affect or the participant's emotions, some focus more on perception, some focus more on values, while still others have a cognitive or "thinking" focus. As stated earlier, it is the *mix* of affective, perceptual, aspirational-volitional (value), and cognitive material that varies according to the objectives of the particular laboratory (Benne et al, 1975). For example, encounter groups focus more on affective material at an *intra*personal level, while T-groups focus more on affective and cognitive material at an *inter*personal level.

Singer and his colleagues maintain that the boundaries between the kinds of groups must be managed by the trainer in order to prevent disorientation of the participant. Boundaries represent the delineation between the end of one thing and the beginning of another. Most boundaries in psychological functioning need to be permeable, that is, they need to be strong enough to delineate the entities which meet, yet permeable enough to allow the entities to integrate. At an intrapersonal level, an example is the need to recognize the difference between a thought and a feeling, yet be able to integrate the two in order to produce congruent behavior. The trainer's job in laboratory education is to keep the focus of the group on the stated level of learning yet allow for sensible overlap with other levels. For example, a program may be designed for learning about group process, yet one cannot learn about group process without understanding the impact of his or her own behavior on those processes and vice versa. Thus, a group-focused program will inevitably include some examination of interpersonal behavior, just as an interpersonally focused program will inevitably include some examination of group dynamics.

Laboratory Education Versus Psychotherapy

Given the above, it is not surprising that the boundary between education and therapy is permeable in many kinds of laboratory training events. The premise still remains that, in the behavioral sciences, laboratory training is an educational activity, not psychotherapy, and not a substitute for psychotherapy. However, the term *group therapy for normals* is evidence of the difficulty that sometimes arises in clearly dividing laboratory learning from psychotherapy (Wechsler, Messarik, & Tannenbaum, 1962).

A closer look at the schema of Singer et al. (1975) will provide a starting point for exploring the question of laboratory training as education rather than therapy. Table 1.1 shows the various kinds of groups and how they relate to the continuum ranging from learning (cognitive and/or perceptual change) to psychological change (altered coping capacity or personality structure).

A Tavistock program would be an example of 1*b*. A Gestalt therapy group would be an example of 1*d*. An Alcoholics Anonymous or a Weight Watchers' group could be an example of 1*f*. Personal growth or encounter groups would be found in 1*c*, and a T-group could be found in 1*a*. In that laboratory education focuses on learning more than on psychological change, groups found in 1*a* and 1*b* are easily placed in the "lab" category. Groups that fit clearly under the category of psychological change are not laboratory education, even if some laboratory training methods are used. The grayest area between laboratory learning and psychotherapy is in 1*c*: the encounter group, personal growth group area. Indeed these programs, when conducted for learning purposes, require the most attention to distress prevention and management.

Even there, however, the laboratory education program can be differentiated from therapy: participants are not called patients (or clients); the trainer's purpose is to facilitate learning rather than psychological change; the action research or "learning to learn" concept is the principal vehicle for learning, rather than, for example, a guided exploration or uncovering of one's formative years. The focus of laboratory education is on the "here and now," and restricts the exploration of behavior to that particular group at that particular time. The trainer's commitment to the participants is for the brief duration of the program, not for the time that would be required for participants to incorporate psychological change into a repertoire of altered responses.

Our Concerns and Hopes

Having defined what is meant by laboratory education or laboratory training in this book, and stating the terms *trainer* and *group leader*

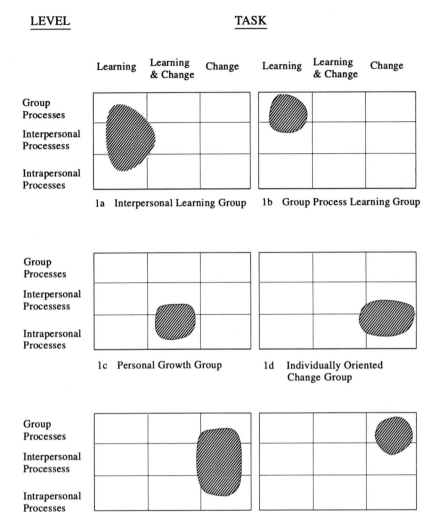

Figure 1.1. Task and Level in the Six Types of Small-Group Events

SOURCE: Reprinted with permission from NTL Institute. Singer, D. L., Astrachan, B. M., Gould, L. J., & Klein, E. B. (1975). Boundary management in psychological work with groups. *Journal of Applied Behavioral Science*, 11(2), 137-176. Copyright 1975.

will be used interchangeably to represent various forms of the group leadership role, we will move to another aspect of defining our playing field.

The authors are concerned that this material might erroneously be used for applications beyond its capabilities. First, the book is *not* a "how to" manual. Such a manual is not possible because all events in the life of a group have to be understood in that specific group's context. Also, many aspects of an individual learner that affect participation in laboratory learning such as life stage, learning style, life problems, race, gender, and history cannot be included in general statements about individual and group behavior. Indeed, we found ourselves vacillating between being as specific as possible in order to be most useful, and being as general as possible in order to recognize the limitations of specific examples. Each person, each group and organizational setting, and each trainer-participant interaction influences the decision about appropriate action. One has to "be there" in order to be specific about interventions.

In addition, this book was written to assist trainers in working with individuals who are experiencing a distress reaction that might lead to a behavioral outcome that has been labeled in this book as a clinical distress incident. The reader should remember that whenever action is described, the focus is on the individual. Many levels of intervention exist in a program: intrapersonal, interpersonal, group, and, at times, the larger learning community. Whenever one intervenes, whether in a crisis situation or not, all levels must be considered, in that all exist simultaneously regardless of which level one chooses to address. We caution readers, therefore, not to generalize our discussion of an intervention with an individual to other levels of the social system, and to keep in mind that our focus is on the individual, even though intervention may be made at other levels.

Finally, we cannot overemphasize that this book is not a substitute for in-depth training and supervised experience. In the area of behavioral sciences, laboratory education is not a precise field. There are many who believe that it is a social movement and should never become a discipline. Indeed, some people believe that such restriction could limit its potential use. However, free entry into the training field creates the inevitable problem that the competence of trainers is variable and often undetermined. Organizations like the Association for Creative Change have established nontraditional certification processes and are worthy of the support of all of us involved in laboratory education. But there are no substitutes for lengthy and disciplined study, supervised practice, and on-going peer review. Thorough knowledge of, for example, theories of learning or education, group development, individual development, and stress are essential. Both traditional and nontraditional assessments can be useful in the quality control of laboratory education. This book does not, by itself, provide adequate information and preparation for preventing and managing of distress in laboratory education activities.

As stated previously, the more affective or "feeling" and intrapersonal or intrapsychic forms of laboratory education have much in common with psychotherapy. Neither the field of education, nor psychology, nor psychiatry has attempted to do the research needed to establish formal training programs for these forms of education. Instead each discipline claims a "piece" of laboratory education. In fact, laboratory education is interdisciplinary, which is why even those who come from rigorous training in a discipline such as psychology or psychiatry are not prepared by that training alone for laboratory education.

Thus, this book assumes an educational rather than clinical group setting even though the relationship to psychotherapy is acknowledged. The focus is often psychiatric but not medical, in that treatment of disorders is not assumed to be the goal of laboratory education even in emotionally intense groups. Hopefully, this book will bridge disciplines and philosophies in the pursuit of advancing individual learning and growth. Rather than arguing the value of academic credentials, arguing the domain of psychotherapy, or the value of experience in the workplace; rather than staking a claim on which group should "own" laboratory education or which group should regulate it, it is hoped that by increasing awareness, knowledge, and skill, readers will remain open to information from any source that might further the advancement of learning. Thus, the serendipity from bridging such groups could be as important as the discovery of the participants in Connecticut in 1946 when a collective, innovative effort produced the behavioral sciences' laboratory method.

2. THEORETICAL FOUNDATIONS

In order to proceed with a discussion about preventing and managing distress reactions in laboratory education, several interrelated concepts must be reviewed and a common exploratory framework established. First, Kurt Lewin's (1951) concepts about action research and the unfreezing-changing-refreezing process that occurs in laboratory training groups will explain the dynamics of the learning process. Second, Hans Selye's (1974) theory of stress will explain the dynamics of the stress involved in learning. Third, Schutz's (1958) group development theory will enable an examination of the individual's stress while learning each of the groups' developmental stages. Finally, some concepts from analytic psychology—transference and counter-transference, and some brief exploration of a few of the defense mechanisms most relevant to training groups—will be discussed.

Action Research and Change

Kurt Lewin was a rigorously trained scientist who, for all of his theoretical orientation, was a major force in the *application* of knowledge. It is no wonder that he focused his work in ways that took action on an immediate problem (racism) in the Connecticut workshop in 1946. Action research is the gathering of information by those who must act on a problem or issue, as compared to scholars gathering research for theory building which can be used by others.

In the case of laboratory education groups, individuals interact in the group setting wherein both individual and group behavior is examined. Research is done or data is gathered on those behaviors (affective, perceptual, aspirational-volitional, or values and cognitive material) and is fed back to individuals who use it to analyze their own and the group's or organization's behavior. Individuals decide upon altered ways of behaving, experiment with it, data is collected, and the cycle keeps repeating itself via the feedback process. The feedback comes from the group members themselves as well as from the trainer or group leader. Controls for reliability and validity are not paramount in action research in that repeatability and generalizability of findings to other individuals or groups is not the point. The individual serves as his or her own control. Learning from the "here and now" of these people in this setting is the point. The task of laboratory learning is to facilitate each person's understanding of issues about her- or himself and about her or his particular situation. People learn to furnish and gather data, participate in analyzing it, and take responsibility for its use. Experimentation with behavior transcends experimental research design, and validation within the group is achieved through consensual decision making in interpreting and using data. As Marrow (1969, pp. 148-149) describes the process, "when the members of a group participate in a program to discover the facts about their own beliefs, the findings they make will stimulate changes in their conduct. The experiences they acquire and share with others—as part of fact finding research makes possible the establishment of new behavior patterns that otherwise would be rejected." This ongoing process of self-inquiry enables the individual, group, or organization to continually adapt to changing conditions and forces analysis of the suitability of present behavior.

Lewin's (1958) conceptualization of the change process that enables learning involves three stages. The first is unfreezing in which the person's present stable state—that is, perceptions, values, thoughts, and feelings about something—is altered or disconfirmed. For example, the action research process in a race relations group may provide data that, when analyzed, disconfirms racial stereotypes. Once the person's previous state of equilibrium has been upset and produces a motivation for change, he or she will seek information about the kind of changes in attitudes or behaviors that are congruent with the new information. The seeking and analysis of information for the purpose of gaining new knowledge, attitudes, values, and perceptions leading to new behaviors is what is known as change. The final stage is refreezing, in which the old (from the frozen state) and the new (from the change state) are integrated into new responses. This is now the refrozen state, which is necessary for the change process to begin again. Unfreezing can be risky in that one must expose one's old responses. Changing is threatening for a number of psychological reasons, including the possibility that one's previous beliefs and attitudes were somehow wrong or inadequate. It also requires experimenting with new responses that are not familiar and involve a period of incompetence.

The Concept of Stress

The laboratory method of learning requires people to open up their thoughts, values, beliefs, feelings, and behavior to public (in the group) examination and personally reconstruct them as they wish and/or are able. Understandably, this learning method can be stressful. That stress level can vary according to the makeup of the individual, the nature of the learning event, and the competence of the trainer.

Although the learning group process may promote stress, it is necessary to acknowledge that it is the individual who experiences the stressful event. It is helpful to have a way to understand the stress process.

In his review of the concept of psychosocial stress, Rutter (1981, p. 323) discusses the historical acquisition of several rather different meanings for *stress*. "Thus, 'stress' seems to apply equally to a form of stimulus (or stressor), a force requiring change of adaptation (strain), a mental state (distress), and a form of bodily reaction or response (that is, Selye's general adaptation syndrome of stress)."

Hans Selye (1974) suggests that the stress response is a demand for action to reestablish the organism's customary state of equilibrium or balance or a return to what, for each individual, is normal. His work provides some interesting guidelines for those conducting laboratory education events.

Not all stress is negative and it can result in several outcomes:

1 growth and desired change—called *Eustress* from the Greek prefix Eu for "good,"
2 no change, or
3 *stress* that can result in a clinical distress incident.

Although change can result from distress, it is not as manageable, desireable, and often not as adaptive as change associated with eustress. There are times when we exceed the limits of our adaptability and feel overstressed (i.e., hyperstress). There are also people who suffer from too little stress (i.e., hypostress) and need more stimulation to be more in balance. Complete freedom from stress is a deadly state, if not, perhaps, death. Figure 2.1 provides Selye's schema of stress.

Selye emphasizes that one should pay attention to individual differences in ability to withstand stressful events without becoming distressed. Indeed, he criticizes the popular stress inventories that are in common use because of their failure to account for individual differences. Individuals often do not understand themselves well enough to avoid distress. Selye refers to two main types of people: "race horses" who thrive on stress and a fast pace and "turtles" who thrive on peace and tranquility. Either type can occasionally mistake their own type for the other and push themselves beyond or below their normal endurance level of stress.

Stress overload is often created when a person whose current life circumstances already strain his or her coping capacity and then meets with an additional problem. In laboratory education that additional problem could be, for example, an awareness of an interpersonal incompetence. Brown and Harris (1978) suggest that an event like seeing oneself or one's situation in a new more negative (even if more real or "authentic") light may trigger the onset of psychiatric impairment, whether in a T-group, a sales role play, or a performance appraisal interview. Trainers who establish group norms that require self-confrontation instead of an opportunity to voluntarily choose it,

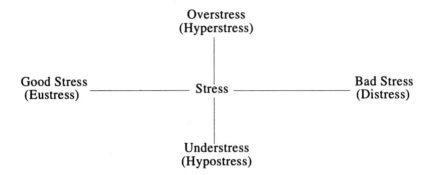

Figure 2.1. The Four Basic Variations of Stress

SOURCE: Selye, H. (1980). The stress concept today. In I. Kutash, L. Schlesinger, & Associates (Eds.), *Handbook of stress and anxiety*. San Francisco, CA: Jossey-Bass. Reprinted by permission.

deprive participants of self-management and the ability to use the coping skills they already possess. This can also trigger deviant behavior in an attempt to reestablish "normalcy".

In addition to one's current "load" of life circumstances, individuals vary in regard to internal factors like temperament, intelligence, values, and cultural background. Some factors are not changeable, such as race, while others are malleable, such as values or ideologies. Many external factors are beyond their control. Examples of these are noise, comfort of physical environment, schedule, work load, travel delays, weather conditions (such as temperature), work space, and availability of resources (e.g., friends or money). The physical environment impacts significantly on human behavior (Resnick & Jaffee, 1982). All individuals are exposed to stressful events and the laboratory learning environment is one such event. The impact of the stress event is altered positively or negatively by the series of internal and external factors leading to the state of stress that the individual experiences. The trainer needs to focus on influencing the outcome in a positive, growth-oriented way so that positive stress (eustress) occurs. The outcome is influenced by the ability of the stressed individual to manage the state, and by other modifiers that affect the equation. The process is a dynamic one, clearly illustrating that not all stress is experienced as negative, and indeed is a necessary component of change.

The general contention is that stress drives the human machine and is, at an appropriate level, a necessary ingredient of successful laboratory learning just as it is in life. Again, Lewin's view of the need for unfreezing in order to explore new options and later refreezing at a higher level of functioning enables us to conceptualize the process. Unfreezing is perhaps the most risky business of laboratory education and calls for management by participants and trainers alike.

The overt manifestation of stress varies greatly from one individual to another. Examples of physiological change due to stress are increased heart rate, dilated pupils, increased muscle tension and perspiration, and shallow, rapid breathing. Headaches, chronic fatigue, and bruxism (grinding of teeth) are commonly induced by stress. Behavioral indicators are withdrawing from the learning group (including drop-outs); exaggeration of one's usual coping mechanisms such as incessant talking, increased smoking, drinking, or sexual activity; changes in physical health (Cohen, 1981) or physical patterns (sleep difficulties), sudden accident-proneness, high anxiety, depressed mood, and, of course, frank psychiatric disorders.

Selye identified a pattern of events in experiencing stress that he calls the *general adaptation syndrome* (GAS). It is made up of three stages. First is the *alarm reaction* in which the organism first reacts to the shock of the stress and then rebounds from it in a countershock reaction. The second stage is the *stage of resistance* in which the organism mobilizes for a longer term reaction to the stress. Third is the *stage of exhaustion* which inexorably follows if the stress is sufficiently prolonged and severe.

While GAS is a biological concept, there are psychological parallels. The energy required for adaptation is not unlimited; undue psychological stress cannot be endured indefintely. Just as biological activity causes wear and tear, psychological wear and tear can accumulate. Adaptation energy does not exist the same way as, say, caloric energy. Selye provides an example of extraterrestrials looking down and trying to understand how a car runs and why it may break down even though it has plenty of gasoline. They soon learn that a car's "driving energy" can be exhausted and the car can break down permanently. With a reckless driver, a car breaks down more quickly but with good driving habits the car has a longer life. In laboratory education, one of the trainer's jobs is to ensure that participants do not drive recklessly.

Previously, the caution was made that a laboratory education experience should not be mistaken for mental health treatment or seen as its substitute. Participants usually do not come to the environment defining themselves as sick or mentally ill, and clarity regarding this issue needs to be maintained. Indeed, Vestre, Greene, and Marks (1978) report no significant differences in psychological adjustment between volunteers for sensitivity training groups and a random sample of nonvolunteers. However, some individuals do enter the laboratory environment at certain critical points in their lives, and these may be unduly weighted with a number of stressful events and they may be inclined toward reckless driving.

Many individuals enter into laboratory education at a time when they are involved with multiple life transitions and may be experiencing significant stress from back-home changes. Indeed, organizational training is often keyed to transition (e.g., new hire orientation, job restructuring, or organization redesign—related, for example, to downsizing, new product introductions, and so on). Some of the stress is from the individual's developmental stage of life, some is from new jobs, new responsibilities, career changes, or from family disruptions. The point is, participants frequently enter the learning environment with a significant pool of stress that will almost certainly be affected by the laboratory experience. Depending on the participants' coping abilities, the additional learning demands may be sufficient to promote distress. This underscores the need expressed in Chapter 5 (Prevention) for trainers to be aware of factors such as the participants' ages, their career roles, emergency contact person (support network), and so forth. In order to have learning occur from the inherently stressful experience of laboratory education, stress must hold the promise of eustress or the joy of fulfillment. Participants are not always aware of their own adaptation responses and may need help in managing them.

Some participants will not have explored stress management techniques and may legitimately look to the group and trainer for coaching. Many individuals have lived most of their lives being quite out of touch with their feelings. They function adequately in their employment and home life, primarily on a cognitive or defended (see Analytic Concepts in this chapter) basis. The difficulty these people have directly experiencing emotions and stress may leave them vulnerable within the group. Understanding some basic principles of stress can help draw our early attention to individuals who use only physical means to express their tension or distress, such as the excessive exerciser, rather than using multiple management activities, or those who exhibit other indicators of overload or inappropriate ways of coping.

With these concepts of stress in mind, we now want to look at some of the unique aspects of the laboratory environment, especially the things that participants import into the groups. Life experiences, strongly held beliefs, values and ideologies, and unresolved but powerful early relationships are material for experiential learning about oneself. Expectations about the laboratory learning event, both conscious and unconscious, and the stage of the participant's own personal development play a powerful part in how the experience is tolerated and understood.

A major way of understanding the importance of these factors brought into the learning environment is to think in the broader terms of ageism, sexism, and racism. Being a single person, disabled, sick, or a minority of any kind within the emotionally intense environment of the group can lead to considerable difficulty. These and other differences within groups sometimes lead to isolation, and to the experience of deviance as compared to difference. It is clear that deviance in learning groups leads to reinforcement of previous coping mechanisms such as regression (see Analytic Concepts) and/or to considerable stress, neither of which may result in a desired outcome. It is particularly important to recognize the reinforcement aspects of groups as they struggle with their development. The group's desire to have stable roles and secure norms may result in behaviors that become exaggerated. A group member who tries to maintain his or her real difference may become singularly uncomfortable. The process may go round and round, using different content, but promoting a circular cause of reinforcement for a member's deviance or deviant behavior. Racial and cultural minorities are particularly vulnerable and represent internal modifiers that trainers need to be aware of and act upon. Prompt action of the right kind may prevent a recreation of societal problems like racism or sexism in the emerging group culture.

The task of laboratory education is to promote growth and change. The process is a risky one for participants and staff, in that individuals need to emancipate themselves from inappropriate defenses, alarm reactions and stress adaptations that they have used for years to make life predictable and seemingly safe. The outcome is largely positive with growth arising from the process of unfreezing and realignment, or change. Factors do exist, however, within some individuals (internal factors) as groups attempt to engage in the collaborative inquiry (action-research) that may lead to clinical symptoms or what we have defined as a *distress reaction*.

Group Development

The third conceptual basis for preventing and managing distress reactions in laboratory education is group development. There are many theories of group development, and their differences are significant in the trainer's understanding of the group process. Unanimity of understanding about how groups form, develop, and terminate is not the purpose of this book. It is enough for our purposes here to say that groups share certain common characteristics that are the need for a task, predictable stages of development, and norms by which they operate.

Importance of the Task

Groups form around a task. There is an old example of an aggregate of people sunning themselves on a beach who are transformed into a group by a shout of "help." By identifying and accepting the task of rescue, the unrelated people in the aggregate are transformed into a group. Laboratory education groups form around the tasks such as learning about behaviors of individuals (including themselves) and about groups. The tasks of laboratory education programs might include the following:

- To increase awareness of one's internal needs, values, and perceptions and to understand their impact on behavior
- To increase group problem-solving skills and techniques
- To understand the effects of individual and group dynamics on group or team effectiveness
- To increase awareness of and sensitivity to emotional reactions and expression in ourselves and others

- To increase awareness of one's managerial style and the effects it has on others' job satisfaction and productivity
- To understand and utilize the concepts and theories of individual and group behavior as a trainer or as a manager
- To increase awareness of the various effects of individual difference such as race, sex, and age
- To increase understanding and competencies in "learning to learn." (action research)

These task or goal statements can be cast in the context of the environment in which the event is being conducted. For example, increasing awareness of and sensitivity to emotional reactions and expressions might be accomplished while pursuing more effective employee performance appraisals or while learning to deal more effectively with customer complaints. The tasks may be well articulated, yet often they are difficult concepts for participants of small group educational events. As will be discussed in Chapter 5, confusion about the learning goals and lack of clarity or agreement about the tasks can be a primary generator of stress in experiential or laboratory learning. It is crucial that group leaders or trainers and participants are clear about and accept the stated tasks of the group.

Stages of Group Development

Laboratory learning groups, like all groups, have defined stages and a developmental sequence. For example, Schutz (1958) expressed this developmental structure with the concepts of *inclusion, control,* and *affection.* His three-part theory assumed the dimensions as basic interpersonal needs that were reflected in recurring cycles within the components of group behavior, as the group moved from formation to a more developed state. Groups begin, form, and grow. Schutz's theory is simple enough to work with, widely known, and sufficiently differentiated to be helpful in discussing distress incidents in the context of the various stages of group life.

The first stage of group development, *inclusion*, is characterized by member concerns about being received, and about how much they wish to be a part of the group. During this initial stage, members are unfamiliar with the other people and/or with the task in that it has yet to be attempted. Because unfamiliarity leads to insecurity, members use defenses and behaviors that were successful for them in similar circumstances. Risk taking is low and cooperativeness is the norm.

When the critical mass of the group has sufficiently (not necessarily maximally) resolved their inclusion needs, the next phase of development becomes the concern about *control* or influence—that is, will they be "on the top" or "at the bottom"? Members test each other, as well as the trainer, to determine who controls whom and how much control each member wants to give to others. Although trust may be developing, power struggles are likely and conflict may be brewing, especially with authority figures such as the trainer.

When control issues have been sufficiently resolved, the group enters the affection stage. This stage can be characterized as "near" or "far" with regard to sentience. Bonds are established between members based upon their common experiences in the group. During this stage, the group is most effective at task accomplishment, and members work together rather than individually or as subgroups. The authority of the group leader diminishes as a pervasive issue.

These stages continually reoccur during the life of a group. When the group faces a threat, it recycles to the control or even to the inclusion stage. As the program continues, the repeated cycles result in increasing cohesion and effectiveness.

One limitation of Schutz's model for the purposes of this study is that it does not emphasize the termination phase of a group. Although ongoing groups will continue to move back and forth between the three stages already described and although temporary groups inside organizations (e.g., task forces) do not preclude member contact after the task force work is completed, laboratory training groups are usually temporary events, and members may never see each other again. Groups end, and that ending can evoke stressful dynamics both for the individual and the group. Saying goodbye, leaving without closure on personal issues, and the anticipation of reentering other environments all present opportunities for learning and/or distress. Distress can be evoked differently at different stages in group life. The inclusion, control, and termination stages are major dynamic elements that should most concern the group leader or trainer.

All groups develop operating norms. Norms are both the conscious and unconscious agreements that are made among individuals in the group, which determine the amount of pressure on people to conform to certain behaviors. For example, a group dilemma may develop when a norm for self-disclosure is set too early in the life of the group. Individuals who feel themselves at risk are placed under undue pressure regarding self-concept or being accepted. Norms regarding member behavior outside of sessions are also established. Eating together or socializing after work hours as a way of establishing group identity becomes common. The development of norms and boundaries gives rise to the dynamics of inclusion or exclusion, (i.e., who is in and who is out) and may lead to emotional tensions in this area. All of us have, in varying degrees, a need for group inclusion. Exclusion is experienced with some stress and a sense of deprivation. The pressure for uniformity can become tremendous and, as a natural corollary, the group pressure to define deviance within the group also becomes greater.

Analytic Concepts Useful for Trainers

Though laboratory education is differentiated from therapy, trainers need to know some concepts from psychoanalytic practice. Those concepts are transference, countertransference, projection, denial, splitting, and regression. The latter four concepts are part of the defense mechanisms that, depending upon their use, help or hinder effective adaptation to the group or learning event. Each of these concepts will be explained and put in the context of experiential learning rather than psychotherapy.

Transference is the unconscious attachment of feelings, attitudes, and thoughts to persons in the individual's contemporary life, which were originally formed around important people in the individual's childhood, especially parents. The tendency is to transfer those early feelings and reactions to people in the present who unknowingly are serving as "stand-ins" for someone else in the past. Transference responses are not rational or based in reality. These responses, which arise for all of us from time to time, can provide a learning opportunity. Conversely, if left unrecognized for what they are (irrational and not based in reality), they can obstruct learning and even be reinforced by the interaction they evoke.

As members of a laboratory learning event interact, positive and negative feelings emerge. Examples of positive feelings are idealization of another or emotional attachment to another. Negative feelings may take the form of hostility, anger or resentment. Transference takes place *between group members* as well as *between members and the trainer*. It is important that the trainer pay attention to both of these levels of transference.

At the trainer-participant level, the trainer must remember that he or she is the most likely stand-in for historical authority figures in the participant's life. If there is no rational explanation for a participant's hostility (for example, the learning event has just begun and for no apparent reason the participant is hostile to the trainer), the trainer must take care not to react to the hostility as if it had validity or to be seduced into conflict. Sometimes it is helpful to deflect the participant's emotional reaction by gently offering an interpretation or encouraging the participant to interpret his or her behavior—for example, "Perhaps we have an example of what is going on with your boss."

Transference offers a moment for learning about the irrationality of the reaction and how that interferes with establishing a more useful and reality-based interaction with, in the above case, authority figures. On the other hand, if the trainer reacts to the hostility *with* hostility (in all probability, triggering an all too well-practiced scenario for the participant), it both reinforces the irrational behavior and allows a nonreality event to interfere with the trainer-participant relationship throughout the event. Moving the emphasis away from the trainer and participant diminishes the probability of developing an unmanageable and unrecognizable magnification of the transference.

As stated earlier, transference also occurs between group members who are stand-ins for authority, love, rejection, and so forth. The trainer who recognizes transference at work in such instances can help mediate conflict more appropriately and not give the irrational behavior that follows the irrational emotions more credence. Again, it is useful to shift the emphasis from the interpersonal interaction to encourage inquiry about what is, in fact, happening.

Countertransference is the unconscious emotional reaction of the trainer or group leader to a participant's transference behavior. It is manifested by the trainer responding to a participant's emotions in kind. In the example discussed above, the trainer who is the object of hostility from a participant's transference would respond with his own hostility rather than interpreting both the participant's and his own emotional reactions. The trainer's response to the participant's transference arouses the trainer's own repressed impulses which further complicates the interaction, turning a learning opportunity into a damaged professional relationship, and interfering with the participant's right to learn. The competent trainer will fall prey neither to irrational idealization nor to irrational hostility by a participant.

It is incumbent upon experiential learning event leaders, especially in events with a high affective focus, that they understand their own transferences, and how they can manage countertransference more effectively. That learning is such a large part of the requirement for psychoanalysts that they undergo analysis in order to more sensitively react to others' emotions. Readers who wish to pursue more in-depth reading about transference and countertransference are referred to *Resolving Resistances in Psychotherapy* by H. S. Strean (1985).

When caught up in the dynamics of transference and countertransference with a participant or a co-trainer, the trainer will likely experience frustration and irritation from a conflicted relationship rather than have an intellectual awareness that might prevent the problem. Once into such a situation, however, a self-aware and knowledgeable trainer will begin to analyze his own feelings, in order to take control of the situation. It is extremely useful to step outside the boundary of the interaction, in order to see and understand it better. For example, a co-trainer in a good staff team may be able to recognize what is happening and help. Seeking out the psychiatrist consultant (see Chapters 5 and 6) can help. It is also a good reminder about the importance of staying in role, in that role differentiation (versus becoming one of the group to meet other needs) can help a trainer step outside the interaction.

An example of unmanaged countertransference occurred when, during a program, a participant left early without notifying the trainer—perhaps as a final defiant and angry act. The trainer and several other participants described the person who left as "angry," "hostile," "looking for a fight, especially with Joe or Frank." In the written report of the incident, prepared by the trainer after the program, the trainer was obviously still angry at the participant and described him in nothing but negative terms. This reverse kind of transference can also occur when the trainer over-identifies with a participant and, for example, is overly protective, or shields the person from useful conflict.

Not understanding one's transference and countertransference reactions potentially harms a trainer's relationship with the participants. This limits the trainer's effectiveness, and may make an unwitting contribution to a participant's relationship difficulties. The trainer is an extraordinarily powerful person in a learning group. The way he or she responds to the emotions of others is often seen by participants as a model of effective behavior. Providing a good model means that trainers must invest in learning about themselves in a rigorous way. Sometimes, when a trainer becomes aware of having gotten into a transference or countertransference situation, an explanation and a simple, sincere apology can be both healing and instructive.

Transference and countertransference can distort one of the primary action-research learning tools—*feedback*. Feedback on reality is potentially useful to the recipient. However, feedback based on transference or countertransference reactions is not likely to be useful because it is not, for the most part, based on the reality of the moment. True, when we experience a transference reaction with another person, that person probably has some of the characteristics we are overreacting to from a past figure in our lives. The problem is that there is a distortion about the degree to which the person has that characteristic and the feedback will be proportionately distorted and unuseful.

The next concepts to be discussed are among the category of analytical concepts known as defense mechanisms. They can be defined as *adjustive reactions*, typically habitual and unconscious, employed to protect oneself from anxiety, guilt, or loss of self esteem. They are, in essence, reactions that have been acquired throughout a person's development, which are automatically employed when the person feels threatened. Many of the mechanisms, particularly the more mature and flexible ones are useful when appropriately employed. For example, denial or refusal to acknowledge a reality is useful when it helps to reduce the negative effects of a traumatic experience. They are only harmful when they enable a person to be unaware of something that needs to be acknowledged, such as feelings of hostility or defects in one's children. The concept of defense mechanisms was developed by Freud and elaborated upon by his daughter, Anna, in her work *The Ego and the Mechanisms of Defense* (1937). The identification of the defense reactions is considered to be one of Freud's major contributions to understanding human behavior and is recognized by non-Freudians as well as Freudians. One resource we recommend for a more detailed description of mental mechanisms of defense is by Laughlin, titled *The Ego and Its Defenses* (1979). The four defenses discussed here are selected because they have a particular impact upon a trainer's competence.

Splitting is a defense mechanism that is best understood in the context of object relations (Klein, 1975). Infants experience objects (including other people) outside them as "good" or "bad." Good objects—ones that bring pleasure—are totally allowed inside the child's emotions (introjected). Bad objects are totally projected—that is, not allowed to become a part of the self—and are consequently made to be part of others rather than self. In this way, we learn how to split ourselves and others into good or bad people. With development and maturation we learn that everyone has good and bad aspects, and to accept the imperfections we perceive in ourselves and others. Trainers as well as participants may reject the part of themselves they see as bad by rejecting the participant who embodies that aspect of self. Helping participants to minimize splitting is an essential training task. A participant who has an instant and strong reaction to another, either positive or negative, may be asked to consider: "What is the 'me' in that person that I am experiencing?"

When co-trainers are leading an event, they must guard against the possibility that participants will split them into "good trainer" and "bad trainer." Although there are various types or styles of leadership, the differences are not so much good and bad as they are addressing different needs. Bales and Shils (1953), for example, describe two types of group leaders. The "task-executive" leader tends to focus on initiating and task performance while the "social-emotional" leader tends more to the emotional needs and tension in the group. Both are needed—neither is good or bad. Splitting provides an enormously valuable learning opportunity for participants, who may leave a group experience with a more balanced approach to assessing others. This learning is begun by assessing what one sees as the good and the bad parts of self, and validating or refuting those long-held inner perceptions.

Projection is the attributing of one's faults to others. This is similar to splitting, in that one may attribute the bad parts of oneself to others, but it differs in that it implies blame. "He made me do it" and "She hit me first" are attempts at justification of one's own faults rather than simply rejecting someone who embodies our bad selves (as in splitting). Projection is the way we excuse or explain ourselves or explain our faulty behavior.

Projection distorts reality and promotes blaming others for one's own inadequacies. People who project a great deal do not easily examine their own motives and avoid introspection. This is best dealt with when the trainer first understands his or her own motives, and by engaging in self-inquiry when attributing a characteristic to a participant. The trainer can assist a participant who is projecting by confronting the distortion and by encouraging other group members to confront distortions as they occur. The use of the "I" position also helps with projection. Typically, the projection is expressed as a statement about another and begins with "You . . ." Asking the participant to restate the observation introspectively as a statement about self can be useful. Certainly trainers need to model this behavior.

As stated earlier, participants and trainers who project may often be accurate in their observation of a characteristic in someone else, because they are so acutely aware of it in themselves. It is not the observation that is of so much concern as it is the source (i.e., is the characteristic in *me* or in *you*?) and the blaming of others for an attribute that resides in the observer. The extreme form of projecting blame outward is to suspect that others, who are the perceived source of a fault, are causing or plotting some sort of harm to the projector. This is a paranoid delusion and not a common defense mechanism. Projection is a special issue in working in multicultural and ethnic groups, since the unwanted parts of people in one culture are often projected to other cultural or ethnic groups.

Denial of reality (i.e., of one's anxiety about reality) is the unconscious defense mechanism that protects one from acknowledging the existence of painful facts that may threaten self-esteem. A little denial is healthy in that one cannot benefit from dwelling on past or present pain and the concurrent anxiety that such thoughts produce. Denial is not self-deception or lying because it is an unconscious process. Because of the unconscious barrier of denial, the person simply does not perceive the existence of the reality. One sees but refuses to acknowledge what is seen; one hears but refuses to acknowledge what is actually heard.

A participant may have feelings of anger toward another participant or toward the trainer, yet be totally unaware of their affect (i.e., suppression). This represents a stage between denial and being somewhat aware—half consciously aware—of a reality and attempting to screen it out. Half-conscious actions like deferring or putting off a confrontation, allowing the group to run out of time, and ignoring opportunities to initiate a discussion are intended to fend off anxiety and often result in increased stress. The trainer needs to build a supportive group that allows the reexperiencing of uncomfortable emotions and liberation from inner restraints that have been developed unknowingly. Reality validation by other group members is an effective approach to a member's denial, in that those other members have usually participated in the same event.

Regression is a return to a previous stage of development in order to avoid the anxiety or other intense effect of the moment. The person resorts to behaviors that are outgrown or out of date. Regression is often neither good nor bad. It is usually inappropriate. A person can regress to childish, even psychotic states, in order to defend against the present anxiety. Intense anxiety can be evoked by a variety of events such as unpleasant emotions (like extremes of anger or joy), fatigue, or physical illness. Because self-esteem is perceived to be in danger, the individual frequently resorts to behaviors that provided relief in earlier, less complicated situations. The reality of external events is thereby ignored or postponed.

An example of regression is provided by the physician who, under stress, chooses to "push the patient's cart" rather than use his or her own special skills and delegate less complicated tasks to others. In a work team, an employee under financial stress may become unusually dependent on the boss's instructions whereas, in other situations, he or she may prefer to be given goals and left alone to achieve the task.

Nonadaptive use of the defenses is most likely to occur when stress is high, for example, during the most intense aspects of inclusion, control and termination stages of group life, or when people are caught up in tense confrontations—perhaps related to transference and countertransference reactions. Rigid and nonadaptive defenses, including those described, can be evoked by the stress induced by poor trainer-participant contracting, as well as by poor boundary management. Participants also import their own life stresses and individualized internal factors.

Thus we see that management of transference and countertransference dynamics begins with the group leader's self-inquiry into his or her own transferences. The defense mechanisms discussed are so commonly a part of every group experience that they warrant highlighting. In addition, the interactive setting is an ideal place for people to learn about their use of defenses. If they enable one to adapt effectively, all to the good. If the defenses are overused (more likely than underused) they serve to distort reality and participants will more likely experience unnecessary antagonism, rejection, conflict, and other unpleasant human encounters. Groups offer optimum opportunities to validate or refute the use of unconscious defense mechanisms and to uncover confusing, oftentimes damaging, transference and countertransferences.

Whether the experiential learning event involves training salespeople, examining corporate managerial styles, or improving members' interpersonal communications, the trainer's task is to create a climate in which people can venture out of past defenses, allow entry of consensually validated reality, and enlarge their options for the future.

Conclusion

This chapter has presented some theories that underlie the trainer's understanding about and ability to deal effectively with participants in laboratory learning groups. Lewin's action research and change concepts explain the here-and-now focus of groups and the cycle of unfreezing, experiencing, or perceiving in new ways and incorporating that into his or her repertoire. Hans Selye's concept of stress alerts the trainer to individual differences in experiencing and managing stress, the need for eustress in learning, and the danger of overload or distress. Today's churning organizational environments make it highly likely that stress will be imported into learning events. Schutz's theory of group development illustrates the phases of stress points that trainers can anticipate. Finally, some psychodynamic theories from analytic psychology enable the trainer to better understand some of the "difficult" behaviors of participants.

As will be discussed in Chapter 8, the theoretical material presented here can serve as a guideline for trainers to assess their readiness to conduct laboratory education groups.

3. TYPOLOGY AND DYNAMICS OF DISTRESS REACTIONS

A clinical incident is a distress reaction severe enough to interfere with the achievement of the participant's or the group's learning goals. The reader will immediately realize that the presence or absence of distress can be a matter of interpretation or dispute. Eustress, as alluded to earlier, is a necessary ingredient for learning and change. An angry outburst by a participant might be seen as "grist for the mill," so to speak, by one trainer, while another group leader may see that same angry outburst as symptomatic of a distress reaction. Who can determine where eustress ends and distress begins?

The level of affective or emotional expression that is acceptable or desirable depends on the goals of the group and on the stage of group development. As mentioned earlier, when a participant's behavior does not meet the norms of a particular group, he or she is seen as deviant, which in itself creates distress for most individuals. Often it is the management of this deviance that determines whether learning and positive change can occur, or whether the deviance grows into a fully visible distress reaction, which then is labeled a clinical incident.

Table 3.1 illustrates the various feeling states, behaviors, and outcomes that result from different stress levels. The trainer's goal is the early recognition of distress so that it can be managed before maladaptive behaviors lead either to further maladaptive behaviors and/or to a disruption of learning.

With the exception of data from well-designed and measured research, statistics about the frequency of clinical incidents in laboratory education are suspect. This is because of the distinct differences between trainers in their perceptions of distress reaction in groups and in their reporting behaviors. Some trainers report the relatively minor reactions that were resolved during the course of the training program while others document only those that remained somewhat of a problem throughout the course of the program or those that continued to evoke concern at the program's conclusion. Should a trainer or group leader not choose to report a distress reaction, it may never come to light. The possibility exists that the trainer who reports more distress reactions is the one who is more aware and less defensive. Such a trainer may be able to detect the warning signs of high stress levels earlier and thus may be in a position to better manage them. A trainer clearly should not be considered less competent *only* because he or she reports more distress reactions than another. On the other hand, when evidence exists that a trainer is lacking in an area of competence and/or is not reporting known incidents, this must be addressed as both a professional and as an ethical requirement.

To obtain accurate data on clinical incidents in laboratory education, the period following such an event needs to be examined as well. Reports that a participant completed a program without apparent difficulty but then developed a serious distress reaction soon after leaving the program, for example, in the airport or a short time after returning home, are not rare. In the group, such participants usually exhibited some signs of distress but they may have appeared to be functioning well enough. Once away from the group, however, they were unable to function satisfactorily. Several hypotheses exist to explain the occurrence of such delayed distress reactions. In some cases the participant may have been able to function fairly

Table 3.1 The Stress Continuum

Stress Type	Feeling State	Behaviors	Outcome
Hypostress	Apathy	Sluglike	None
Eustress	Tension Excitement High energy Sense of well-being	Alert Actively involved Focused Creative Energetic Working within group norms	Growth—New adaptive behaviors Reinforced adaptive behaviors Mild regression to adaptive behavior from childhood
Distress	Inappropriate or prolonged: •Anxiety •Dread •Irritability •Anger •Confusion •Depression •Panic Accident proness	Agitated Disruptive Unfocused Bizarre Incongruent with group norms Accentuation of existing maladaptive behaviors Physical complaints or illness Sleep and eating disturbances Severe regression and psychosis Withdrawal Intense clinging Getting drunk or high	Appearance of new but maladaptive behaviors

well in the group because the group lent its strength to her or him. Once the group and its supportive structure disbanded, the person was unable to manage his or her emergent distress independently.

Another theory is that these group members muster all their emotional energy to put up a solid front in the group for fear of what it might mean, for example, to their self-esteem or career if they "fail" in the program. Once back in their safe surroundings they can then afford to give themselves "permission" to lower their defenses, allowing the anxiety to surface. Thus they begin to exhibit distress because they know that their therapist, family, or others close to them will support and care for them. Another possibility must be considered—namely, that the trainer simply does not sufficiently heed a participant's distress signals and thus fails to take the appropriate steps needed to alleviate the distress in the important termination phase of the group.

Classification of Distress Reactions

In human relations training, a commonly used tool to characterize knowledge about a person's level of awareness and how that person presents him- or herself to others is known as the *Johari window* (Luft, 1963), named after its two originators, Joseph Luft and Harry Ingham. A variation of this handy systematizer is used here to organize the discussion about distress reactions.

The Johari Window of Distress Reactions (Figure 3.1) divides all distress reactions into four groups or quadrants depending on who perceives the distress reaction. For example, does the individual participant as well as the trainer or other group members know about his or her distress (known distress) or does the participant hide the distress or maladaptive behavior from others (hidden distress)? Blind distress reactions are those, for example, wherein an individual sees oneself and his or her deviant behavior as appropriate but may react intensely if the group expresses perceptions of deviance or tries to alter that behavior. In unknown/displaced reactions neither the individual nor the group are aware of the psychological distress. The distress is displaced from the psychological realm into the physical realm thus manifesting itself as a medical problem. In medical practice, despite the obvious nature of some physical health problems, their interpretation as expressions of distress are woefully infrequent. It is remarkable, for example, that individuals treated for slashed wrists in an emergency room are often referred for surgical, but not psychiatric follow-up. Group leaders do well to keep in mind that medical illness in a group member may be due to excessive, albeit unrecognized, psychological distress.

The clinically trained reader may disagree about where a particular distress reaction was placed in this adaptation of the Johari window. This

	Seen by Self	Not Seen by Self
Seen by Others	I. Known uncomplicated anxiety complicated anxiety and depressive states examples —anger —irritability —withdrawal —sadness	II. Blind personality dysfunction = "difficult people" psychosis examples —over defensiveness —dramatization —passivity —paranoia —delusions —tirades
Not Seen by Others	III. Hidden uncomplicated anxiety and depressive states complicated anxiety and depressive states examples —alcohol and drug abuse —gorging/not eating —irregular sleep or insomnia —promiscuity	IV. Unknown/Displaced psychosomatic disorders accidents examples —unexplained illness —not being open to interpretation —risk taking (stunts)

Figure 3.1. Johari Window of Distress Reactions.

is to be expected because different degrees of severity can move a disorder into a different quadrant. Also, subgroups of a disorder, for example of the psychoses, may better fit into a different quadrant. In spite of these difficulties, we hope that the classification scheme presented here will provide the nonclinician with a better grasp of the variety of distress reactions present in groups, information on how they may or may not become manifest, and also in a very general way which types of distress reactions respond best to specific forms of interventions. Let us examine the various distress reactions in more detail.

Known distress reactions (Quadrant I) are generally anxiety states or states of depression. Mixtures of both states are common. Anxiety is an internal state of apprehension and unusual tension, sometimes evidenced by anger. Depression is a despondency of such magnitude that things seem hopeless and there is little expectation of their getting better, sometimes evidenced as irritability. Known distress reactions fall into two groups: uncomplicated anxiety and depression, and complicated anxiety and depression.

Uncomplicated anxiety or depressive reactions are feelings that an individual experiences and acknowledges as they are experienced during the life of the group. These anxiety and depressive reactions can range from mild to severe. Complicated anxiety and depressive reactions, on the other hand, are those in which the psychological distress has resulted in significant physiological changes (loss of appetite, insomnia, or excessive fatigue and sleep) or in significant behavior changes (temper outbursts, missing group sessions, or incessant talking).

In that Quadrant I anxiety, depression, and anger states are known by both the afflicted participant and the group, they are generally the easiest to manage. These problems can be talked about openly and appropriate strategies may be collaboratively developed. Also in milder forms, uncomplicated anxiety and depression most closely resemble eustress and may be seen by a trainer not as distress but simply as an appropriate stress reaction in a new and demanding environment.

Hidden distress reactions (Quadrant III) can be uncomplicated when the individual is aware of the psychological distress yet is unwilling to disclose it and when there are no significant physiological or behavioral expressions of it. Or, hidden distress reactions may be complicated when they are of such magnitude that sleep and appetite are significantly disturbed, or more importantly perhaps, when the afflicted individual tries to avoid the unpleasant feelings and resorts to addictive behaviors. It is unlikely that addictive behaviors or eating disorders begin de novo during the course of a laboratory program. They are usually imported into the setting by the participant. The stress of laboratory education, however, can bring about a relapse of addictive illness or can bring about excessive drinking, experimentation with drugs, food binges, or inappropriate sexual behaviors. These behaviors, of course, can have more severe consequences than the uncomplicated hidden anxiety reactions.

Laboratory education is a stressful event for most participants because it takes significant amounts of energy to be fully present in the group. It is therefore not surprising that a distressed participant who tries to hide his or her anxiety, depression, anger, or addictive behavior may use up excessive amounts of his adaptive energy and, therefore, move into clinically significant amounts of distress. In the case of addictions, for example, the afflicted individual by necessity will have to isolate himself from the other group members in order to gain time and space for engaging in his addictions. Frequently, insufficient sleep is the result. This factor can aggravate the participant's distress level, as well as disturb his engagement with the group, thus resulting in a deviance-reinforcing vicious circle. Moreover, should the behavioral concomitants of hidden distress reactions become so blatant that they are out in the open, a great deal of shame and guilt will be generated that will further add to the intensity of the distress.

Hidden distress reactions are very important because they are likely to erupt as significant clinical problems. They become known distress reactions if their intensity is allowed to build outside the awareness of the group and the trainer. It is, therefore, in the best interest of all participants and will provide them with an optimal learning environment if the early subtle clues that identify participants in distress are detected by the trainer. Careful monitoring is crucial, especially of the more introverted participants, those who miss meals or come late to sessions, or those who isolate themselves from the group's social events. These individuals may be candidates for hidden distress reactions. Participants who are minorities in their group either because of race, language, culture, gender, age, or disability or who choose to live away from the majority of the laboratory community, are also more likely to develop hidden distress reactions. As stated in Chapter 2, feedback with minority group members needs to be monitored especially carefully in order to prevent distortion from transference and projection. Otherwise the stress level of these individuals may increase, with the effect of raising the group's stress level as well.

Blind distress reactions (Quadrant II) are characterized by dysfunctional personality styles and psychoses. Participants who see "other people" as the problem or behave in ways that are self-defeating without knowing that they themselves are part of the problem, are exhibiting dysfunctional personality styles. Such individuals lack "outsight"—that is, sensitivity to the impact of their behavior on others.

Psychosis is a disorder involving at least intrapsychic chaos in which one's thoughts and feelings are inappropriate to the situation. Psychotic behavior is difficult to deal with rationally in that the person's thinking process is not operating in accordance with the reality of the situation. A prime example of this is psychiatrically disturbed thinking of a paranoid nature in which others' benevolent or neutral motives and behaviors are interpreted and experienced in a negative way. The paranoid individual sees others as untrustworthy and deceptive and finds it necessary, therefore, to protect herself or himself. Other examples of psychotic thinking include claims of much greater accomplishments or status than are true—for example, delusions of grandeur. A psychotic individual may hint at or suddenly announce that he or she has extraordinary talents or powers or that he or she is a millionaire with large holdings in various countries or that he or she is an accomplished writer, a personal friend or aide to the nation's president, a visitor from another planet or even God incarnate. Denial, projection, and grandiosity, which are common characteristics of psychosis, account for the "blindness" of this syndrome.

Although manifest behaviors of personality dysfunction and psychosis are apparent to others, the affected participant is usually unaware of his or her difficulty. Anxiety of psychotic proportion and mood disturbances, such as depression are also frequently involved. First-time, acute psychotic episodes are sometimes apparent to the disturbed individual. In such cases, not only is the disorder a known stress reaction, it is frequently associated with readily observable intense anxiety or terror.

Blind distress reactions are quite visible in the group and rarely go unnoticed, but they often are written off as the "participant's problem" and explained by the trainer as inevitable, thus absolving the trainer from responsibility. This interesting phenomenon can lead to poor management of the distressed participant. Participants with dysfunctional personality styles can evoke high frustration and anger levels in trainers and in other group members.

Overly dramatic styles may be interesting for a while but are then seen as excessive or attention-seeking, subsequently the participant's emotional expression tends not to be taken seriously. Participants who exhibit passive, dependent, clinging behaviors generally are offered support by at least some group members until they, too, become exhausted by the constant emotional drain. Passively aggressive participants, overly controlling or demanding ones, and those who are very rigid in their behaviors may be ostracized by the group. This in turn is likely to increase their dysfunctional interpersonal style and isolate them further. Explosive emotional outbursts or tirades may actually frighten the group and generally do not elicit sympathetic or empathetic responses from those witnessing the eruption. Such behavior also tends to severely limit interaction with others and increases isolation.

It is generally true that participants who enter the group with grossly dysfunctional interpersonal styles will exhibit these behaviors as the group progresses through its various stages. Within categories of personality dysfunction affected participants will have predictable perceptions and responses to the group experience (Torgersen, 1980). The degree of expression of a dysfunctional personality style depends, however, on the early recognition and management of those behaviors by the trainer.

Of the psychotic behaviors, paranoid psychotic behaviors occur most frequently. Psychotic individuals may show anxiety in panic proportion or extreme withdrawal and suspiciousness in order to shield himself from the imagined ill will and imagined plotting of all people around them. Probably because of their severity as well as their instructional value, psychotic reactions predominate in the literature as case examples of psychiatric casualties in sensitivity training (Glass, Kirsch, & Parris, 1977; Higgitt & Murray, 1983; Kirsch & Glass, 1977; Sale, Budtz-Olsen, Craig, & Kalucy, 1980). Although a cursory review of the literature might therefore suggest otherwise, psychosis is fortunately relatively rare in laboratory education (Ross, Kligfeld, & Whitman, 1971).

Whenever it does occur, however, it is a very disruptive and unsettling process, not only for the individual afflicted but also for the remainder of the group. Psychiatric intervention, as discussed in Chapter 4, is required to assess the severity of the difficulty and to provide the necessary psychiatric treatment. Participants who suffer a psychotic decompensation—that is, individuals who use primitive defenses or have severely disturbed identities and, therefore, become unable to function personally as well as in the group—generally require medication. Usually a person in this condition is not able to care for himself or herself properly and often does not eat or sleep appropriately. Hospitalization may be required.

Unknown or displaced distress reactions (Quadrant IV) are of two types: psychosomatic illness and accidents. Psychosomatic illness includes such conditions as abdominal complaints, various pain syndromes, and minor infections. Symptoms are often poorly defined and a medical examination may be indicated. Generally the sufferer is not aware of the reason for the illness and is not open to an interpretation that his or her illness may be a distress reaction in disguise.

Accidents resulting in physical injuries that occur during the course of a group are a different matter. The dynamics that lead to them are more accessible to exploration. A well-timed, appropriate remark by a trainer may stop risk-taking behaviors, when, for example, during their free time group members might be tempted to perform stunts to show off their real or imagined talents. Although it would be easy to dismiss such injuries as "just accidents," this perspective is shallow and keeps trainers from attempting to prevent these injuries. Physical risk-taking behaviors can occur at any stage of the group life but are especially likely to occur during the control stage of the group when members compete with one another. In our experience, not feeling as personally recognized by the trainer as other group members are imagined to be has precipitated risk-taking behaviors in some participants in the trainer's presence, and thus led to accidents.

Because medical illness and accidents are possible distress reactions, all medical illnesses and emergencies should be reported as clinical incidents. Also, trainers are encouraged to ask all participants at the beginning of a group experience (the opening session) to report any visits to local physicians or health clinics during the course of a program. The cases presented in Chapter 7 illustrate many of these types of incidents. Although rather extreme, these cases boldly demonstrate the various typologies discussed above.

Dynamics of Clinical Incidents

Based on Brazelton and Freedman's (1971) work with temperament types in newborns, Spitz's (1946) description of anaclitic depression, and George Vaillant's (1977) discourse on adaptive styles, there is a growing consensus that people have little choice as to which type of distress behavior they exhibit. Group participants import into the group their specific coping styles; these styles are based on innate temperaments that have been progressively modified by life experiences. As stated earlier, some people react to stressful situations primarily with anxiety, others become depressed, while others become combative. Although possibly accentuated, the distress response that a participant exhibits in a group setting is the same distress response that he or she exhibits in everyday life when circumstances bring about an *internally* similar sense of insecurity and vulnerability. That is precisely the value of the group experience: It serves as a microcosm of daily life and is therefore a laboratory for learning about individual and group responses.

Infants who experience poor mothering, whose needs are not met in a nurturing way, withdraw, eat poorly, and lose interest in their environment. These same people as adults, when others challenge them, tend to become depressed and hopeless and give up rather than fight for their rights. Such hopeless states can be evoked not only in difficult real life circumstances but amazingly the tensions and ambiguities of group life also can bring them to light, even in the brief course of a laboratory education experience.

Traumatic childhood experiences predispose individuals to more intense distress reactions and, therefore, to clinical problems. Although there is some evidence to the contrary, it is the currently accepted theory that most dysfunctional personality styles (which compose the bulk of blind distress reactions) are the result of grossly inadequate nurturance in the early months and years of child development. The ability to see the deprived, misguided, and abused child behind the annoying blind distress behaviors (the person behind the behavior) will enable most trainers to be helpful to these participants, rather than add to their psychological dysfunction.

T-groups as well as other relatively unstructured learning groups have one thing in common: They set up dynamics very similar to those that the child encounters in his nuclear family. Being included, cared about, and accepted are issues of prime importance to the growing infant, which literally determine the infant's survival. When a group member does not feel accepted by others during the inclusion stage of group development, the feelings evoked by rejection or perceived rejection may recapitulate feelings of panic and fear of annihilation that an infant seems to experience when abandoned. The resurgence of such primitive dreads from those early years, when reason and understanding did not yet prevail, can rise to clinical proportion unless ways are found to decrease the vulnerable person's stress level.

On the other hand, some return to childhood reaction patterns and behaviors is expected in T-groups and similar laboratory learning groups, and generally is not of clinical importance. When participants engage in "Look at me," "Watch me," "Pick me," "Like me" behaviors, they are behaving normally. Limit-testing behaviors such as, "How late may I be before you set limits?" or, "How much may I monopolize the group before you will stop me?" are predictably seen in groups for at least brief periods of time. Regression, the return in adulthood to reaction patterns that were appropriate for a young child, was discussed under defenses in Chapter 2. Regression is commonly seen in all phases of group development and is part of the process of unfreezing which is a necessary ingredient for growth and change. There appears to be an optimal level of regression that will vary from participant to participant and that should not exceed the group norm. Too much regression is likely to be seen as a clinical problem, while participants who are unable to allow themselves to regress at all are often those who do not find their experience in the group very meaningful. Also, as discussed in Chapter 2, transference reactions in groups are common: The male group trainer as well as other male group members are frequently seen in the same light as father was seen, and a female group trainer or participant is likely to be perceived similarly as mother. As described above, this process can lead to distress if the participant transfers inappropriate negative feelings from a childhood relationship onto a person in the group. Countertransference holds the same problems for trainers who are reacting to a participant's transference inappropriately.

Conclusion

Although eustress reactions and distress reactions in group participants may at times be hard to distinguish and although various trainers differ in what they consider a distress reaction, distress reactions can be classified through the use of the *Johari Window of Distress Reactions*. The Johari Window of Distress Reactions divides distress reactions into four groups: known, hidden, blind, and unknown/displaced ones, based on whether the distress is perceived by the self or by others or by both or by neither. This classification system highlights important differences between the categories, with implications for appropriate prevention and management techniques.

Most clinical incidents are traceable to imported, dysfunctional, maladaptive styles and to personality styles that are the result of many variables of which temperament (innate) and childhood experiences appear to be major determinants. Those early experiences underlie the behaviors of participants during each stage of group development. Readers are reminded about regression, which is both beneficial to growth and learning in experiential groups, as well as potentially the basis for distress reactions and clinical problems. Transference reactions and countertransference are again raised as possible problems in distress management, especially if the transference is a negative one.

4. RECOGNIZING DISTRESS REACTIONS

A trainer's ability to recognize distress reactions early is the cornerstone of a safe laboratory education experience. Most, although not all, clinical incidents in groups are preceded by distress signals from the vulnerable participant. Recognizing these signals and finding ways to respond to them in a timely and appropriate way may prevent the development of a full-blown psychiatric condition. When a distress reaction is detected early, before it reaches clinical proportions, resources can be summoned to either prevent a clinical incident or to attenuate the severity of such an incident.

As explained in Chapter 3, not all distress reactions are visible to others, yet it is the trainer's responsibility to be constantly on the lookout for such hidden distress reactions. This is not an easy task. Yalom and Lieberman (1971) described in their article on encounter group casualties that group leaders were generally not able to predict by the end of the group which participant would suffer a distress reaction as a result of the group experience. Instead, other participants had a much better sense of which fellow group member suffered distress during the course of the group or was psychologically hurt by the group. This is a very disturbing finding, especially in that the group leaders that were studied were leaders chosen because of their experience and competence in leading their particular type of laboratory education group.

Knowing that the group leaders under study were unable to correctly identify retrospectively which group members had suffered psychological damage from the group, it stands to reason that these same group leaders were not recognizing clues to emotional distress in their group members during the course of the group. Yet fellow group members apparently were able to do so. One can only speculate about the causes of this finding. If one assumes that participants and group facilitators had the same data (i.e., observations of the behavior of the vulnerable group member during the life of the group) by which to assess the stress level of a participant, then, in Yalom's study, the group facilitators and the fellow group members obviously interpreted distress clues differently.

This might indicate that the group leaders were hardened, so to speak, to watching groups form and disband and witnessing participants struggle for inclusion and control, or whether to disclose aspects of themselves or how much to disclose. Fellow group members, on the other hand, can identify very acutely with the anxieties surrounding these issues in that they are struggling with them as well. Perhaps it has been a long time since the group leaders, or trainers, have been participants themselves and they have forgotten about the stress of being a group member.

Maybe those trainers did not have the clinical training that would allow them to fully appreciate the power of projection and negative perceptions on self-esteem, mood, and rational thought. On the other hand, it could be that some group leaders have such a strong need to be helpful, positive change facilitators that it is too threatening to their own self esteem to acknowledge that (a) not everyone benefited from the group experience and that (b) some developed emotional distress because of the experience. Is it too painful for some leaders to acknowledge that they are not omnipotent and that, in spite of laudable intentions, damage was done? Or were these leaders so absorbed with making the "right" interventions, or with needing to be seen as brilliant, that they were unable to carefully track distress clues in individuals as they occurred? Perhaps they discarded distress signals as "growing pains" and assumed that because they themselves are capable of handling emotional upset generally in a constructive way, everybody else should be able to do so likewise.

There is, of course, the possibility that fellow group members had a greater data base by which to judge each other's stress level. Yalom's study was conducted at Stanford with undergraduate students. These students in all likelihood had contact with one another outside of the groups and therefore may have had more information about one another that could have made it easier for them to accurately indicate which fellow participants felt emotionally hurt by the group experience. Unfortunately, Yalom's study did not address these various possibilities and their relative merit. We therefore do not know why these group leaders were less accurate than the participants in assessing distress. The purpose here is to better equip group facilitators to detect high emotional stress in participants by looking at all of these possibilities and offering ideas about how to make groups safer.

Distress reactions can span the entire spectrum from being indiscernible by the trainer to being so blatant that nobody can miss or deny their presence. This chapter is devoted to helping trainers sharpen their skills in recognizing the various manifestations of distress so that there are no complete surprises when deviant behavior is encountered.

Anxiety and Depression

By far the most common distress reactions are anxiety and depression. In fact, they are probably fundamental to all distress reactions. By definition, anxiety and depression are intrapsychic experiences and as such are not always observable. However, depending on the coping style of the individual, behavioral clues are generally present and can be picked up by an aware trainer even though an individual is trying to hide their presence.

Anxiety states occur when a participant experiences physiological alterations in his or her body secondary to an excessive adrenalin release. Following a frightening thought, the body produces large amounts of the hormone adrenalin, which in turn results in a number of possible physiological alterations. These alterations can include an elevated heart rate and blood pressure, accelerated, more shallow or more irregular breathing, larger than normal pupils, and tighter muscle tone with or without trembling. Changes in skin color from pallor to flush are common.

Trainers can discern some of these changes even across the room if the anxiety reaction is intense, while subtle reactions may be apparent only if the trainer is in close physical proximity to the distressed participant. Some anxiety states, usually those that are milder, cannot be detected in a program unless the participant chooses to make them known. However, sweaty palms or cold hands may signal a distress reaction to a discerning trainer during a casual hand touching. Rapid speech, a hoarse voice, fidgeting, frequent trips to the bathroom, physical clinging to others or sitting in a closed position (legs crossed, arms folded) are other clues. Often the individual may look tired and yawn excessively if the distress reaction has interfered with sleep. Skipping meals may signal that the individual's appetite has been reduced by the anxiety reaction. When a trainer recognizes these signs of adrenalin release he then has to make the often difficult judgment—am I seeing a reaction that is beneficial (eustress), or am I looking at the beginning of a significant distress reaction that needs to be managed to avoid the disruption of learning?

To help with the diagnostic dilemma, careful tracking of the participant's behavior is needed both when the group is in session and during free time. Other staff (if available) can help with some of the tracking, in fact they may already have useful information in regard to the participant's behavior in other settings. Should the concern persist, a check-in round can be used. A check-in round is a structure used frequently in groups to quickly give everyone the opportunity to express how they are feeling and what their needs and concerns are at a particular point in time. The expectation is that every member of the group gives a one or two sentence update on themselves.

Another way to get more information would be, of course, for the trainer to talk informally with the participant in question. Sitting next to the participant at lunch, walking with that participant to the meeting area will provide the trainer with an opportunity to ask, "How is it going for you?" "How are you doing?" The participant will appreciate the personal attention and will generally come forth with enough information to help the trainer decide if there is distress and how severe it may be. This time together can also be utilized for building a relationship between the participant and the trainer, which is so crucial for success both in the prevention and management of distress reactions.

Panic and Memory Loss

Although most anxiety reactions are nonspecific, three types will be described in more detail because of their striking presentations that require skillful trainer management. Hyperventilation, panic attacks, and global memory loss are three specific types of anxiety reactions that we have encountered in small group work. Let us take a look at them one at a time.

In some people the normal rise in respiratory rate that accompanies the outpouring of adrenalin in anxiety states is exaggerated to such a degree that it upsets their body chemistry. Uncomfortable physical symptoms can arise from hyperventilation, which if not recognized for what they are, can cause the participant to experience even greater anxiety. The participant may worry that something terrible is happening to him or her because suddenly he or she has feelings of numbness or tingling in the extremities, feels dizzy, is short of breath, and may have heart palpitations. If the hyperventilation is not stopped the participant may faint, have muscle twitching, or muscle spasms.

Although there are no absolute number of breaths per minute that constitutes "hyperventilation" (different people have different baseline respiratory rates) the trainer can readily recognize an elevated respiratory rate if he or she just remembers to watch the frequency of chest movements of the participant. When the participant's breathing is fast, his color is good and there is no chest pain, yet he describes all or some of the symptoms listed above and appears to be anxious, the trainer can assume that the participant is hyperventilating. Once the problem has been recognized, it is then easy to manage.

At times anxiety reactions can reach panic proportions. When in that state, all of the physical signs of anxiety are accentuated. So intense are the symptoms that the individual is convinced that he or she is about to die or to go crazy. Because of the magnitude of the physiological and psychological arousal in panic states, the individual usually cannot hide the symptoms from the group should they occur while the group is in session. Panics are therefore almost always known distress reactions, especially if it is the first panic attack in the person's history. The individual may not be able to be alone and literally cling to another person for safety until the episode has subsided. Persons who have gone through such a panic attack describe the experience as the terror one might expect to feel if one were pushed out of a flying aircraft without a parachute. Needless to say, while experiencing a panic attack people are extremely emotionally upset, may cry, talk incessantly, and move about frantically, needing the proximity of someone they trust. Fortunately panic attacks last only for a few minutes and are definitely over in less than an hour; however, fear of another attack can leave the individual highly upset for a prolonged period of time.

A more rare type of anxiety reaction should be brought to the reader's attention, because it is known to be associated with emotional distress and, therefore, can occur in affective learning groups. It is a disorder that arises abruptly with little or no warning. Again, because of the magnitude of the dysfunction, this disorder falls into the category of known distress reactions. The affected individual, generally over fifty years old, suddenly loses recent memory and experiences total amnesia of the immediate emotional stress and of the preceding events. New information cannot be retained for a period of six to eight hours. The group member will look fine but will suddenly ask such basic questions as, "Where am I?" "What am I doing here?" or "How did I get here?" Although answers are given and may momentarily orient the participant he will have to ask the same questions over and over again because the answers given are quickly forgotten. Except for the loss of memory the participant is mentally intact and continues to think rationally. Return of memory is gradual and begins with more distant events. Interestingly enough the circumstances that led to the amnesia may never be recalled.

Depressive states very frequently fall into the group of hidden distress reactions. An individual may choose to disclose his or her feelings, which then, of course, would change it to a known distress reaction. Most states of depression lead to behaviors that look like the opposite of anxiety states—instead of being in a state of excessive arousal, the person is slowed down mentally and physically. Unlike anxious participants who may create opportunities to talk even when not appropriate, talking may become difficult for the depressed person. The depressed participant is likely to move slowly, give yes or no answers whenever possible instead of elaborating, may become totally silent, may stay in bed and be late for or even miss the group session completely. Other depressed participants while physically in the group may not be really aware of what goes on around them. Instead, the depressed person is intensely preoccupied with himself or herself and what he or she perceives as his or her hopeless state. The trainer may notice that the participant does not laugh about things the group finds funny and, of course, a depressed participant may cry easily.

Professionals involved in work with anxious and/or depressed clients in clinical settings may be quick to point out that depression and anxiety frequently occur together in the same person, especially when the client is suffering from what is called an agitated depression rather than from the retarded depression described above. This is certainly true, yet it is beyond the scope of this book to instruct the reader in the details of clinical diagnoses. However, one piece of the clinical assessment of anxious and or depressed patients can have relevance to the trainer in laboratory education: Any anxious or depressed state that is coupled with a definite sleep or appetite disturbance is likely to be of greater intensity or significance than one that is not. Asking the participant about sleep or appetite disturbances can therefore help the trainer in estimating the severity of the distress. It is important here to understand that depression can lead to both marked increase or decrease in appetite and sleep. Deviation in either direction of a person's baseline should be considered significant.

Dissociative States

States wherein a certain function of the mind becomes isolated from the remainder of an individual's experience are called dissociative states. Dissociative states are mentioned briefly here because they can also erupt during the course of a laboratory program and may frighten the trainer who is not aware of their existence. In that the affected participant usually does not feel distress while in a dissociative state, these disorders have been listed in the blind quadrant of distress reactions. Two different types are described here.

Depersonalization and derealization are sometimes called altered states of consciousness. In such states a person may feel detached from his or her mind or body and feel like an outside observer or an automaton or may feel like a participant in a dream. Most people have experienced such states momentarily at some time in their lives. Trance states in hypnosis are akin to dissociative states, as are some drug induced states. These episodes can be brief or prolonged. T-group members may not feel too threatened by a member's brief dissociative episode. In fact the group members may not even be aware that it is occurring. Prolonged depersonalization states, on the other hand, can be quite stressful and disruptive.

Fugue states are another type of dissociative state. Fortunately, they are rare. A person in a fugue state may suddenly drive off without prior plans to travel, will forget his past including his identity, and then assume a new identity for an indefinite period of time. Situations as seemingly simple as driving to a doctor appointment might arouse unconscious anxiety sufficient to trigger a fugue state in people predisposed to this expression of stress.

Addictive Behaviors

In that the reader is probably familiar with the various signs of intoxication and can recognize a drunk person when in the presence of one, the emphasis here will be shifted to how to raise one's index of suspicion when confronted with alcohol abuse that a participant is trying to hide. Clues may include a group member's nodding off during group sessions or not participating and instead apparently daydreaming. These behaviors, along with finding that same participant late at night in the bars, perhaps even with people outside of the laboratory learning community, can help the aware trainer to recognize the distressed participant. Drug abuse is even more difficult to detect and generally remains a distress state hidden from the group and the trainer.

Binge eating as is found in bulimia, with or without subsequent purging through vomiting or laxative abuse, can occur in normal weight, underweight, or overweight people. It is a secretive activity that would almost never come to light in the course of a program. On the other hand, anorexia nervosa, even though the participant will try to hide it, may be detectable. The afflicted person is generally a younger woman who is unusually thin, who exercises strenuously and yet misses meals or eats only salads or other low calorie foods when she does eat. Typically the afflicted participant will spend an enormous amount of psychic energy trying to find ways to engage in the usually secretive behaviors in order to conceal their existence. This then leaves little in the way of emotional reserves to deal with the stresses of group life. Thus such group members become very vulnerable to overt distress reactions when they find themselves not being included in the group or confronted by other group members. Some participants, in order to be less exposed to the scrutiny of others, may choose to live in a hotel away from the rest of the laboratory community because it is easier for them to hide maladaptive behaviors. Paying attention to living arrangements can thus be an additional way to identify participants at risk.

With the sexual revolution of the sixties, the sexual behavior of many people changed. Many people allowed themselves to become sexually involved with new people in their lives. In that laboratory education groups often led to great emotional intimacy, it was not unusual then that participants also chose to become sexually intimate with one another. In the late 1970s and early 1980s and especially with the advent of AIDS, there has been a drastic change in societal mores. These societal changes have made an impact upon the norms of sexual behavior among group participants; casual sex appears to have become uncommon. Nowadays group members who become sexually involved with one another during the life of a group are more likely than in the past to be evidencing vulnerability. These participants possibly deserve extra attention from the trainers.

Dysfunctional Personality Styles

Personality dysfunction behaviors, which comprise the majority of problems in the category of blind distress reactions, are behavior patterns of long-term duration that generally cause the person significant impairment in social or occupational functioning. As such they will come to light during experiential groups as well as during more cognitive groups in which cooperation around a task is necessary.

Individuals with personality problems are the "difficult people." Because of hypersensitivity to rejection or perceived rejection they may be emotionally volatile, have angry outbursts (even angry tirades), attack others, be demanding, expect special treatment, be intrusive and disruptive. Their impulse control may be so poor that they come late to sessions or miss sessions, flirt with other group members, do not eat or sleep properly, and perhaps abuse alcohol.

Depression is common and suicidal gestures or self-mutilation (cutting) may occasionally be seen. Others may be overly controlled or rigid and without trust. They cannot disclose their vulnerabilities and show little empathy when others are in pain or distress. They may harbor ideas that they are better than anyone in the room and therefore remain aloof. They respond to positive feedback but negative feedback may make them very angry and elicit counterattacks or sudden departures from the group because of their excessive anger, shame, or sense of utter humiliation.

Overly dramatic, "histrionic" behaviors can be equally distracting to the work of the group. They are more commonly seen in women. Generally, histrionic women dress seductively and exhibit excessive emotionality. Because she needs constant reassurance and praise, such a woman may quickly pair with a man for support, leaning excessively on him and taking both their energies away from the group work. Emotions are expressed freely and with great intensity. Examples include excessive sobbing, perhaps over a minor hurt or a small mishap, or temper outbursts in response to minor frustrations. Such a person may stand out early in the group's life because she may engage prematurely and excessively in hugging and touching before it becomes a group norm.

Participants who have dysfunctional personality styles can be difficult for trainers to cope with because they so often attack a trainer's competence directly or indirectly and disrupt the group by being unreasonable and insensitive to the needs of their fellow group members. If a trainer has had a lot of negative experiences earlier in life, these difficult people may evoke his or her usually well-controlled negative transference reactions, which can then result in overreaction to the participant or in an untoward countertransference reaction. The trainer's overreaction can further escalate the annoying behavior in the participant and perhaps push it to clinical dimensions. Trainers therefore need to be very careful when they find themselves becoming upset with a participant. It behooves them to analyze the degree of their discomfort and to see whether it is proportionate to the provocation. When countertransference reactions occur, a co-trainer can be extremely useful in helping the trainer recognize his or her inappropriate responses to the participant.

Psychosis

Psychotic disorders were briefly described in Chapter 3. In addition to delusional disorders—that is, when people hold on to false beliefs in the face of rational evidence to the contrary, and the more frequently occurring paranoid disorders—a third type of psychotic disorder may present itself. It is characterized primarily by disorganization of thoughts. Apparently functional people may suddenly begin to ramble incoherently or talk about hearing voices when no one is speaking; that is, they may disclose auditory hallucinations. Their faces may not express much emotion or the emotion expressed may not be congruent with their thought contents. Grooming may be poor and they may suddenly talk to themselves and engage in nonsensical behavior. When a psychotic break occurs in a group, other members generally become alarmed and frightened and the trainer will need a good support system in place in order to be able to not only deal with the distressed participant but also deal with the group effectively. The majority of psychotic states are blind distress reactions, meaning that the individual is not aware that his or her mind is not functioning properly. Case 2 in Chapter 7 describes a case of a smoldering psychosis that did not become fully manifest until the participant tried to return home.

Timing of the Distress Reactions

Though distress reactions may occur at any time in the life of the group, they are frequently not manifest until the middle of a week-long laboratory program or later. However hints to the distress can often be picked up during the opening session of the lab. In fact, of all time frames in the course of a laboratory, the opening session is probably the most fruitful setting in which to identify potentially vulnerable participants. To the aware trainer, vulnerable participants stand out in the opening session because they exhibit extremes of the normal entry behaviors.

For example, certain participants may be more shy and more withdrawn than the rest of the group while others may be overly engaged and ask many questions even though the information has been provided already through handouts or announcements. Then there are those participants who are dressed very differently from the rest of the group members or those who wear inappropriate clothes. Anybody who looks poor physically should be noted. It is of great importance that trainers pay careful attention to the first remarks and disclosures by group members in the opening session because they can be extremely revealing. The new group members may talk, for example, about their fear of entering the group, announce that they were "sent" to the group, or that they just came to have a good time on the golf course.

Whenever possible, if the group event is a large one, all staff members should be present at the opening session to have as many eyes and ears available to tentatively identify those participants who may be more vulnerable. Frequently, when the various observers pool their observations, the same individuals emerge as being somewhat deviant from the norm. In our experience these same individuals often arouse concern during the life of the group and at times indeed turn out to be participants who develop clinical distress.

All of the above distress reactions have to be differentiated from unfreezing, the state wherein a group member has decided to let go of an old behavior pattern and experiment with a new one. Unfreezing may mimic deviant behavior. One difference is that an unfreezing state is usually short lived and responds quickly to feedback. The experienced group leader will recognize it as regression possibly in the service of personal growth and make room for the experiment without shutting it off prematurely.

Certain distress reactions appear to have predilections for certain group stages. Participants who had traumatic childhoods with insufficient nurturance, the loss of their mother, or other significant losses in the early years tend to be vulnerable to depression. For them the inclusion phase may feel especially stressful because once again they fear that they may not be "good enough" or "valuable enough" to be accepted by others. Also, if the group has gone well for individuals susceptible to repressive feelings and the affection stage of the group has infused them with the glow of finally having found people who accept them as they are, termination may be a serious event. For such individuals, resurrecting the feelings of utter sadness and hopelessness that they had experienced when love was lost for them in childhood can be devastatingly painful.

The control phase of the group is likely to be the hardest on those participants who had to struggle for survival in childhood and on those who were involved in heated sibling rivalry or other rivalries early on. The more severe personality disorders probably will have difficulty in all stages of group development but are likely to become more activated during the control stage of the group.

For individuals who are very rigid and are afraid of the expression of feelings, especially the positive ones, the stage of affection is likely to be the most threatening one. They frequently cannot engage in the process of unfreezing, yet they feel ostracized when they are not included in psychological warmth and intimacy. For others the affection stage may be stressful because the group norm of physical touching (which frequently emerges then) may bring them in conflict with cultural mores, or even some long harbored prejudices against being physically close with people of color, homosexual individuals, and so forth.

The type of emotional distress reaction a group member may experience as he or she moves through the various stages of the group depends upon temperament and previous life experiences, with brain chemistry being another major determinant. The trainer has no influence on any of these last three variables, but might help significantly by being alert to potentially vulnerable participants and by spending the needed extra time and energy to contain excessive stress which otherwise could lead to a clinical incident.

Conclusion

Early recognition of vulnerability is a cornerstone of safe laboratory education. The phenomenology of distress reactions was described in detail in order to allow trainers to recognize subtle signs of distress and to be familiar with the more severe forms of emotional dysfunction. The importance of trying to identify vulnerable participants in the first session of a group event was stressed in the hope that clinical incidents may be prevented during the laboratory. Although any distress reaction can occur in any stage of group development, certain categories of participants are susceptible to stage-specific distress reactions by virtue of their psychological predispositions.

5. PREVENTION

Managing distress in laboratory learning begins with preventative measures. Most of these should be taken even before the group is convened. Preventative measures include (a) the written program description and the psychological contract it implies, (b) the kind and quality of information requested on a program application and the uses made of that data, (c) the preparation of the staff both individually and as a team, (d) the trainer's awareness of his or her professional "style," (e) the initial stage setting or the program's opening session, and (f) the identification and preparation of a clinical consultant in case such assistance is needed during the learning event. This chapter examines each of these prevention measures in detail.

Program Description

The importance of clearly articulating the aims and methods of a program cannot be overstated. For example, if a corporate training manager does not clearly state, in announcing a performance appraisal training event, that self-awareness and interpersonal skills training are two of the program objectives, and that personality inventories followed by discussion of personality profiles, or unstructured role plays, such as simulations of appraisal interviews will occur, he or she should not be surprised if a participant accustomed to "classroom" methods becomes distressed. As noted earlier, experiential learning using action-research is more stressful than traditional lecture-discussions, and if participants are unprepared they may employ their customary coping styles, which may not work. More importantly, participants come to laboratory programs for a variety of reasons, some of which are unclear even to them. Thus, the program description in the promotional brochure or announcement must be succinct and straightforward in order to eliminate any early misconceptions.

Sponsoring institutions sometimes offer broad, nonspecific program descriptions because the program has not yet been designed or to allow trainers greater personal freedom in program design and conduct. There is also a temptation to include all possible audiences in order to increase attendance, but this can also serve to confuse participants who, after all, are placing themselves and their psychological development in someone else's hands. The description serves to establish a psychological contract between the sponsoring institution and the participants. Like every educational event, a laboratory program should have learning goals. These goals, not the trainer's personal interests, should be the object of the program activities. Above all, trainers must beware of managing the boundary of personal growth kinds of programs in order to prevent them from becoming a gathering of people engaged in psychotherapy—even if some of the participants, for reasons mentioned earlier, are eager or willing to do so.

It is incumbent upon the trainer to behave in ways that are congruent with the program contract and the predictable dynamics of groups. For example, a group-process program becomes insidiously confusing if the trainer intervenes mostly at the interpersonal or intrapersonal levels and vice versa. This illustrates how the program description serves to establish a psychological contract between the trainer and the participants.

The trainer in laboratory learning is like a manager who specifies a task (learning goal), clarifies roles and responsibilities in carrying out the task, contracts with others regarding these activities, and continually monitors adherence to the contract (Singer et al., 1975). As in any management activity, part of the trainer's monitoring task includes assessing her or his own personal predispositions and needs and not permitting them to transcend the commitments of the contract.

By describing the program accurately and requiring trainers to meet the contract as written, sponsoring organizations can contribute significantly to the prevention of distress. These actions aid prospective participants in selecting appropriate programs and in knowing what to expect, so they can manage their behaviors in ways that are appropriate for the program. The concept of "informed consent" applies at all stages of laboratory education (Malcolm, 1973). "If responsible public education can teach prospective encounter group members about what they can, with reasonable accuracy, expect in terms of process, risks, and profit from a certain type of group then, and only then, can they make an informed decision about membership" (Yalom & Lieberman, 1971 p. 30). This statement applies to all affective educational events—not just encounter groups.

Application Form

Once a program has been designed and described, interested participants need to provide the information requested on the application form. In laboratory training, the information potentially available on an application is more important than in educational events of a strictly cognitive nature, and some of the questions asked on the form are of increased importance. The importance of screening individuals has already been introduced by mentioning the unknowns regarding the motives or goals of applicants entering particular programs. Sponsoring organizations, therefore, should help applicants articulate their learning goals. Vague goals such as "to learn to be a better manager," "to learn about groups," or "to learn about myself" should be clarified through follow up contacts. It is of critical importance that the staff members who process applications are skilled in detecting participants enrolled in the wrong program, or in the right program at the wrong time.

Because of the potential for emotional disruption in laboratory training, some programs, such as T-groups, and personal growth programs, require disclosure of psychotherapy or significant life stress at the application stage. If an applicant has a history of psychotherapy, especially a history of a psychiatric hospitalization, the nature of it needs to be determined in order to decide if the program would be appropriate for him or her. Psychiatric hospitalization would alert one to the higher risk of psychosis or severe depression. On the other hand, a history of psychotherapy in the past, if used for managing less severe life issues such as divorce or career change, generally does not indicate that the applicant is at present a high-risk candidate for a distress reaction. Some therapists believe that asking an applicant to secure his or her agreement for participation in a program is not congruent with the psychotherapeutic relationship and, therefore, not a reasonable practice. However, our view is that both the sponsoring organization and the applicant are well served by this request. Even though some applicants present inaccurate or even dishonest data, the institution usually secures better information than it would otherwise have on which to make a decision. In addition, many therapists wish to participate in the decision about their patient's or client's engagement in laboratory learning. Certainly therapists have an interest in the welfare of their patients or clients, and their input is of great value.

This discussion does not imply that applicants secure "permission" from their therapists to attend a program. Ultimate responsibility for that decision, as well as for one's behavior in a program, is the responsibility of the individual participant. Rather, there is a need to discuss the learning goals. In this perspective, a discussion with the therapist can be helpful for the applicant's preparation for the learning event and his or her therapeutic process as well.

The more affective the focus of the program (e.g., personal growth programs) the more relevant is the current degree of general life stress to the application process. A self-rating stress scale on the application form, with a request that applicants assess themselves may produce information useful not only for screening but also for program design. In their study of screening for T-groups, Stone and Tieger (1971) report that one positive effect of the screening was the leader's response. "Some of the leaders who participated in the screening process felt much more confidence in their leadership roles. They knew the participants and could better anticipate initial responses in the group, and they felt reassured that the likelihood of potential disruptive reactions had been lessened."

As illustrated in Cases 5 and 6 in Chapter 7, questions about current medical problems and current types and amounts of medication taken need not be looked upon as intrusive. On the contrary, they can yield extremely valuable information, not only in regard to understanding a participant's life stress but also in an emergency, when that type of information could actually save a participant's life. Also, a question about special dietary requirements may be appropriate—especially in international programs.

Other information on the application form can be of great value in planning a laboratory program. For example, age might be used to get a general feel for the life-stage issues that may be at work for an applicant. Armed with knowledge of human development, the trainer can more thoughtfully assign individuals to groups for various activities. Race or gender, for example, may alert trainers to some developmental stage issues and "difference" issues, such as mentioned in previous chapters, that may need to be anticipated in planning specific activities.

Other differences are important to notice. If the majority of participants are sponsored for a management skills program by their organizations but one person is not identified as affiliated with an organization, the trainer may be dealing with someone who is either unemployed—an increasingly frequent occurrence with organizational downsizing—or who does not identify with an employer. That participant's needs may therefore be at variance from those of everyone else in the group. Participants from foreign countries (another increasingly frequent occurrence) may import not only a different culture but also may have limited ability to become included, or to interact, because of language difficulties. Their religious days (Holy days, Sabbath, etc.) may affect program scheduling. Different dietary requirements may make their meal times stressful. Disabled persons may find that others are uncomfortable with their handicap. Entry and inclusion may be quite awkward without some facilitation by the trainer.

The nature of the applicant's relationship to his or her emergency contact person (who should be identified on the application form) can provide information about the participant's support system. A fifty-five year old male or female who lists mother or father as the emergency contact person is not necessarily lacking in personal support, but such data will enable the trainer to be more alert for other indicators that may predispose this person to distress.

It is a good idea to include on the application form a question about which, if any, laboratory programs the applicant has attended previously. An applicant may list a number of personal growth programs whereas the program for which application is being made now is a management skills program. In this case, especially if the applicant's learning goals are vague, a trainer should consider the possibility that the person is seeking something other than simply management skills, which are the goals of the program as stated in the program description. In cases in which applicants have attended previous programs with the sponsoring organization and in which there was a history of a distress reaction or other indicator of concern (e.g., the person left a program "because the boss called him back home"), the trainer should be apprised.

If responses on applications are rambling or incoherent, it is a good precaution to contact the applicant in order to get more data. Also, a trainer is well advised to take note of the presence of several persons from the same organization or department who may import a subgroup culture or particular norms into the new group. It has been our experience that T-groups, for example, comprised of colleagues are almost always more stressful and clinical incidents are more likely to occur. Departmental cultures in the same organization can vary greatly and the dominance of one subculture in a group can significantly affect interaction and conflict.

Applicants who do not live-in during a residential program should be noted by the trainer because they have the additional burdens of daily travel stress, longer hours, and not being included in some out-of-group activities or discussions. Each item on the application form seen separately may not yield the information that the data as a whole can provide in order to form some hypotheses.

Even though a trainer can usually do no more than make assumptions at this point, application data does enable the staff to make significant decisions about the appropriateness of specific program activities that have been planned, group or subgroup formation, and the particular staff skills that should be assigned to particular participants. The applications should be reviewed on-site as part of the staff planning process. The review, especially the analysis of application data, is best done as a group, so all staff members can be aware of warning signs. Collective staff interpretations may well contribute to program design or modification and conduct.

All of the above are good reasons why completed application forms *must* be available to the staff before the program begins. Last minute applicants are sometimes more predisposed to distress reactions, both because of less thorough screening in the rush to meet the deadline, and because applicants who have self-management problems are more likely to begin a program with this kind of behavior. It is far better to postpone participation than to include a distressed participant who will not be able to participate fully or whose behavior will diminish the program experience for others.

Finally, it is advisable to look for the applicant's most recent laboratory learning experience. For logistical reasons, participants sometimes wish to enroll in a series of back-to-back programs. A teacher may apply for a series of programs because summer is the only time he or she is free to participate. Or, a person traveling from a great distance may wish to compact as much learning as possible into a few weeks or months because of travel costs. For whatever reason, concentrating too much affective learning into a continuous block of time is very unwise. The more affective the program focus, the less advisable that programs should be taken in rapid succession. The nature of emotions requires that they be experienced in natural cycles of intensity with ebb and flow. Putting too much emotional learning into a short period of time precludes learning and increases the chances of creating chronic stress leading to a distress reaction. This is as true for staff members who conduct successive programs as it is for participants.

The Staff Team

Although a training staff member may work alone in the small group, T-group, or whatever the subdivision of a larger group may be called (e.g., the search group in a Tavistock program), he or she must not be working independently of other staff members. That is, activity in one group must be appropriate when compared to what other trainers are doing in their groups. Using Singer's model again, one trainer should not be using an intrapersonal change model while other trainers are using a group learning model. The program should not have, for example, a T-group in one room and a Tavistock search group in another unless by design and stated purpose.

Conflict between staff members must be sufficiently managed to prevent staff dynamics from contributing to distress reactions. This can happen unintentionally or unconsciously. A staff member may, for example, displace anger on a vulnerable participant by mentally blocking on a participant's name and devaluing him because his name is similar to a disliked staff person's name.

Trainers and other staff members need to discuss the learning contract among themselves prior to conducting a program. At this time, they can clarify their differences. Good interpersonal relationships among staff members, like all other good relationships, require time and work. All of this means that staff members must invest adequate time in developing their team prior to opening a program. Although it may appear "experienced" or "competent" to arrive the evening before a one week residential laboratory program, produce a familiar design over dinner and begin the event the next morning, it is not professional. Staff members who work together frequently, know each other well, and have a good relationship may need less time to prepare for a program. Conversely, those who do not know each other well or who have relationship problems with each other require considerably more time to prepare. The foregoing caveats are true also for staff pairs who co-train in the same group. All programs require staff team development. Without it, participants are placed at higher risk of distress.

The Trainer's Style

The variable over which trainers have the most control and for which they must assume most responsibility is their own behavior in a learning event. A major factor in the prevention and management of distress in laboratory programs is the facilitation approach, or style, of the individual trainer.

A trainer must be aware of his or her style prior to a program and use this self-awareness appropriately.

Lieberman, Yalom, and Miles (1973) discussed the impact of leader or trainer behavior on participants. A particular training style, if oppressive, can have negative effects on participants not only in terms of their learning but also in terms of their self-management. Trainers who are distant, aggressive stimulators (Lieberman, Yalom, & Miles, 1973) or who are highly controlling in their group management were found to have more distress reactions in their programs. The highest risk style is the charismatic leader who is an intense emotional stimulator—for example, one who establishes a norm that every group member must participate or disclose at the same intense level in order to be part of the group. A high-risk training style, in combination with an unclear contract, interacting with a participant whose learning goals are either inappropriate to the program or unspecified (so that they cannot help to manage his or her psychological boundary) and a person who is experiencing unusual life stress is a powerful combination for producing "deviance" as a distress reaction. Under these circumstances, how can it be said that the distressed participant embodies psychopathology? This is an especially appropriate question given the educational rather than therapeutic orientation of laboratory education.

The norms from which participants deviate are largely in the trainer's control. To what degree is conformity to the leader's own style the measure of a participant fitting into the program? How far can the behavior of participants deviate from the leader's style before being seen as inappropriate, and eventually causing them to be seen or to see themselves as deviant? A leader who is excessively forceful and pushes his style on a group challenges a participant with a very different style to employ intense contrary behaviors or emotions, thus distorting his normally adaptive style to one that looks very deviant. Suddenly a participant finds him- or herself in the minority role with all the attendant emotional isolation. He or she will be placed under tremendous pressure to conform, or else face being excluded. Both alternatives lead to further anxiety, anger or depression with increasing feelings of inadequacy. Constructive learning cannot occur in such a climate and the participant may leave the program abruptly. The tragedy is that the deviant group member generally sees him- or herself as the cause of the problem and a failure, when in reality the oppressive or domineering leadership style of the trainer was to blame.

The Opening Session

This is an extremely important part of the program that is often seen by trainers as simply getting started, "warming up," or getting ready for the real learning to come. Ideally, this session can assist people in their inclusion, provide a forum for discussing some good tips for stress management during the program, and set norms that will facilitate early detection and intervention with participants who may become distressed.

The opening session should provide people with a nonthreatening opportunity to present themselves to others and interact in a confidence-building way. For example, a management program would probably not open in the same fashion as would a personal growth program, in that the kinds of activities appropriate to the latter would go "too far too soon" for the more conservative norms of most managers and their environments. Going too far too soon may keep some managers from participating with ease, thus they will feel unsure about their acceptance from the very start.

Staff have an opportunity to discuss the need for good self-management, that is, proper sleep, exercise, and avoidance of overeating and over-drinking. While late night "rump sessions" are engaging, they can be not only debilitating but also may cause work that should be done inside the group to get done outside of sessions, thereby diluting program effectiveness. Participants need to be told that any medical problems that arise, certainly any doctor visits while at the program, must be reported. These visits may be distress indicators, in addition to being problems of a physical nature, that need staff attention. Staff should also advise participants that they are available for out-of-group talks, especially if a participant finds that the group experience is not meeting learning goals or is not going well. The trainer's job is a 24-hour one during laboratory education events.

Should a participant, during an opening session, indicate that the program seems to be of questionable fit, the trainer needs to tend to the inquiry immediately. If a person is mismatched with a program, an early opportunity to leave should be provided. Indeed, exit needs to be facilitated. For example, a referral or application of the tuition to another program can remove a financial barrier. Legitimizing the departure to the participant's boss (even discussing it together with the boss) can remove an organizational barrier. A participant who feels he is a captive to a program will not be able to learn and may reduce the learning for others.

Experience has taught us that it is wise to state during the opening session that, should anyone, for any reason, need to be absent from a session or need to leave the program altogether, staff must be notified. Depending on the nature of the event, participants may be told that they will be searched for should they be absent and fail to inform staff in advance. This announcement is especially important in programs with a strong affective focus. It conveys to participants that the staff is totally committed to their welfare and focuses on the responsibility of each participant to be direct and open with the staff. Many potentially severe distress reactions have come to light earlier than they otherwise might have because of this group policy (see Case 7, Chapter 7).

The Clinical Consultant

More will be said about the use and roles of a clinical consultant— preferably a psychiatrist—in Chapter 8. As part of the prevention chapter, it is enough to say here that having a clinical consultant who can be reached during a program and who is adequately familiar with the goals and methods of the program is good professional practice.

Ensuring the availability of this resource does not imply an expectation of trouble nor does it imply that the program is high risk. Indeed, it is advisable that even company training departments keep a liaison with the medical department for organizational programs. The authors' experience—both organizationally as well as clinically—has been that medical departments are pleased to be included and will usually try to be extremely helpful.

In order to be of best use, the clinical consultant needs to be briefed as stated above and, equally important, the staff-consultant relationship and expectations need to be established before the program begins. A clinical crisis is not the time to introduce yourselves to each other! More will be said about the clinical consultant in Chapter 6.

Conclusion

Distress reactions occur in laboratory programs for many reasons that can be prevented. Programs must be described adequately, enabling the psychological contract between the participant, the program, and trainer to be clear. The special importance of a detailed application form was discussed especially for programs with a strong affective focus. The trainer must reconfirm and carry out the program contract and the trainer needs to ensure that his or her style does not result in norms to which an individual cannot, or will not, conform. The staff team itself must be built. If there is strife between different team members, this can be a source of distress for the participants.

Much useful information about an individual participant's imported stress level can be gathered at the very first session of a program. Using that information can help trainers focus their attention on a vulnerable participant as well as convey some useful tips on managing stress, which will hopefully reduce the risk of escalation into a distress reaction. Finally, it is good professional practice to have available a competent clinical consultant who is familiar with the program and who has established a relationship with the staff.

Rarely is a distress reaction the result of any single ingredient. More often, distress is caused by a confluence of several ingredients. With care, many precipitants of distress can be identified and prevented.

6. MANAGING DISTRESS REACTIONS

Distress reactions range in severity from very mild to severely disabling. In that people are such multifaceted organisms, no two individuals' distress reactions will look exactly the same, nor will they have identical meanings. The type of interventions chosen by laboratory trainers will therefore vary from one incident to another and should be created to fit the specific situation.

The purpose of this chapter is not to provide a list of specific interventions for specific types of distress reactions. The "cookbook approach" is not effective. Instead, our intention is to provide a structure by which small-group trainers can think through and discuss intervention options when they have to manage a participant's distress.

To guide the reader through the various intervention options this chapter will first present a classification model as the theoretical underpinning and then move into the more practical section on managing distress reactions in participants. Aggressive outbursts and psychotic reactions are of special concern when they occur in groups because they tend to arouse anxiety in trainers and because of their potentially serious consequences. Their management is, therefore, described in more detail in the section on Enforcing

Healthy Group Norms. A discussion of the role of peer and psychiatric consultation in the management of clinical incidents follows. Although this topic is extensive enough that a separate chapter could have been devoted to it, we decided to make it an integral part of the management chapter in order to emphasize that consultation is indeed a cornerstone of the safe management of clinical incidents. The chapter will conclude with guidelines on ways in which to handle distressed participants in the termination phase of the group who may need follow-up after the group.

The Cohen and Smith Intervention Cube

Any discussion of managing distress reactions would be incomplete without introducing Cohen and Smith's (1976) three-dimensional framework of various intervention options. In brief, the model involves analysis of group leader interventions along three dimensions:

1. intensity (low, medium, high),
2. level of focus (group, interpersonal, individual), and
3. type (conceptual, experiential, structural). (See Figure 6.1.)

Although this model was not specifically constructed for the classification of interventions that best decrease distress in small groups, it does lend itself very well to that purpose.

The *intensity* of an intervention is determined by the degree of intended confrontation, not by the confrontation itself. Confrontation, according to Cohen and Smith, is a psychological, intrapsychic interpretation of behavior. A high-intensity intervention would be one which increases awareness significantly and which is sharply focused. A comment directed at an authority-challenging individual group member about his or her behavior, pointing out that his or her nearly indiscriminate challenge of the group leader is excessive, and then interpreting it as possibly being the "Angry Child" breaking through is an example of a high-intensity intervention. Although high intensity interventions are more commonly made at the individual or interpersonal level, they can also be used at the group level. Choosing an intervention of the intensity that will best decrease stress is an important tool for trainers in preventing and managing clinical incidents.

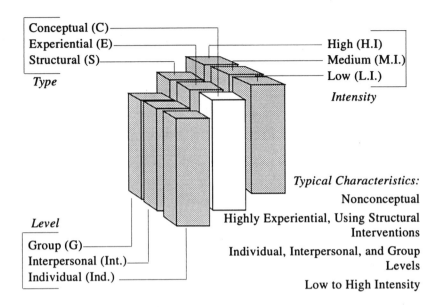

Figure 6.1. Group Leader Intervention Options. Reprinted from Arthur M. Cohen and R. Douglas Smith, *The Critical Incident in Growth Groups: Theory and Technique.* San Diego, CA: University Associates, 1976. Used with permission.

No explanation is needed in regard to the various levels of intervention. The level is determined by the trainer's estimation of placement accuracy, and effectiveness. And, group level intervention remains a group level intervention even if an individual member may perceive it as directed at him- or herself.

In severe distress reactions, most interventions are appropriately placed at the level of the individual. At that time, the needs of the group may conflict with the distressed individual's needs. A creative challenge for trainers is to find a balance within their intervention repertoire between individual participant and group needs. There are times when such a balance cannot be maintained because the needs of an individual participant in distress are more compelling. We suggest one basic principle for trainers and administrators of laboratory programs: no intervention is acceptable if it places an individual participant in real danger, either psychologically or physically.

As indicated above there are also three different *types* of interventions. The *conceptual intervention* is one in which the group leader expresses an idea, concept, or thought. Here, cognition is primarily involved. Conceptual interventions are excellent tools for decreasing distress provided that the distressed group member is able to process cognitive input at that time. An *experiential intervention*, on the other hand, is either direct expression of feeling by the trainer about an observed behavior or an encouragement of group members to express their feelings. Because experiential interventions focus on emotions and may thus heighten intensity, it is important that they are used especially skillfully when emotional distress or overload already exists. The division between conceptual and experiential interventions is not to be seen as an absolute one in that thinking is, of course, accompanied by feeling and feelings have rational thoughts associated with them.

Lastly, *structural interventions* are activities or exercises introduced by a trainer. They can range from highly verbal concept (task)-oriented ones to nonverbal, nonconcept-oriented ones. Structured experiences usually fall into the latter group. They are a special type of intervention introduced by the trainer that focuses attention on emotions or feelings. What Cohen and Smith call structured experiences have been called nonverbal exercises in other chapters of this guide. A trust walk (one participant leads another who is blindfolded on a walk) is an example of a structured experience. Dividing the group into quartets around a task, or while the group experiences an impasse, asking all individual group members to stand up for a minute and think of something that each one could personally do to get the group unstuck are examples of concept-orientated structural interventions.

Thus, not all structural interventions are structured experiences, but all structured experiences are structural interventions. Structured experiences are rarely appropriate in managing distress. In fact, if not used with care, nonverbal exercises may create distress. The task-oriented structural interventions, however, have a definite place in the management of distress. In the case studies in Chapter 7 many of the group leader interventions have been analyzed using the Cohen and Smith Intervention Cube to give the reader an opportunity to heighten his or her understanding of its use.

Management of Medical Illnesses or Accidents

Trainers are not usually directly involved in managing medical illnesses or accidents. A trainer, however, is responsible for ensuring that the sick or injured participant receives prompt medical attention. Should the participant have to leave the laboratory, it behooves the trainer to be sure that realistic travel plans are made so that he or she returns home safely. When family members or friends cannot meet the patient upon arrival, an escort from the sponsoring institution might be needed, for example, to help the patient to the nearest hospital. In cases in which the illness is thought to be short-lived, and the participant is expected to return to the group in a day or two, it is important to monitor his or her progress at least daily, through personal visits by the staff. Sometimes a distressed individual does not recover as quickly as expected. This may represent an occasion in which the trainer will want to guide the individual to leave the laboratory early if too much was missed. Even though the group leader may suspect that an accident or medical illness has a strong psychological foundation, in other words is a Quadrant IV disorder, it is rarely wise to burden the participant with that presumption until he or she is well again. Even then dealing with the cause of psychosomatic illness is best left in the hands of a competent clinician who can have more long-term contact with the patient.

Practical Strategies for Managing Distress Reactions in Participants

Once a distress reaction has been recognized, whether at the opening session of a laboratory or during a later phase, the immediate goal is to contain or decrease the stress, in order to prevent it from escalating into a more severe problem. The familiar concept of the vicious circle (Wilkinson & O'Connor, 1982) operates in groups and in their distressed participants.

Although numerous examples could be cited, only one will be presented to illustrate the point.

Bob, a white, balding male in his late forties came to a T-group laboratory "to become a better manager." In the opening session of the laboratory Bob stood along the wall while other participants sat on chairs. He was a very quiet participant. Actually, he had spoken only once in the first two T-group sessions. (When everyone in the group introduced themselves by name and said why they had come to the program, Bob also briefly introduced himself.) Throughout, Bob appeared tense and uncomfortable, shifting his position frequently. He arrived late for the third T-group session. Participants sitting next to him smelled alcohol on his breath. Bob again did not actively participate in the session. In that the group was preoccupied with a participant who had been crying about having recently lost a child, no one commented on Bob's apparent sleepiness.

The next morning Bob could not be found. He had left the program. When his trainer finally reached him, Bob reported that he had a back problem and had increasingly developed pain from the long trip to the laboratory site. He therefore could not sit during the opening session, and when he finally did sit down later in the day, he remained in a great deal of pain.

Unfortunately, he had forgotten his pain pills and, therefore, resorted to alcohol to help himself cope. When he could not sleep that night on the soft mattress in his hotel, he decided to return home by limousine and plane.

Fortunately, he arrived home safely.

This brief vignette is a sad example of a missed opportunity in helping a participant whose distress might have been discerned from the very beginning of the program. Because his distress had not been noted, he progressed into a dysfunctional state. The group totally ignored him, while their attentions focused on another, more expressive participant. Bob had not realized that, even though it was Sunday and all stores were closed, he could have received a prescription for his medication from the program's back-up psychiatrist.

The reader will recognize that at least three of the "Do's" in T-group programs described in Table 6.1 had been ignored. The staff had not announced to the participants that they wanted to be informed about medical problems as they arose. Additionally, the trainer had failed to make personal contact with each group member quickly, preferably within the first twenty-four hours of the program, either within or outside of the group. Had he done so, he probably would have learned that Bob needed a firmer bed and a different chair to sit on during the group. Bob was a shy person who lived alone and was not in the habit of relying on other people for help. Finally the staff had not announced that anyone who planned to miss a session should inform staff of their intent to do so. Thus a simple problem (Bob had forgotten his pain medication) grew through the dynamics of a vicious circle into such severe stress for Bob that he could not remain in the laboratory.

Many stress reduction strategies are available to the trainer; those commonly used are listed in Table 6.2 and are discussed below.

Give Support

Being recognized, heard, and understood are conditions all people require in order to maintain a positive mood and good self-esteem. It is the rare person who retains emotional and physical well-being even though he or she is rejected or ignored by all. Humankind honors such persons as martyrs or saints. People differ greatly, however, in the amount and frequency of affirmation they require from others. Some adults, like children, need to be affirmed daily by whomever they come into contact with, while others are able to maintain emotional stability in spite of only sparse or rare affirmation by an individual whose opinion they value.

Groups are not immune to scapegoating, an ubiquitous phenomenon in human systems (Stafford, 1977). A group may reject or ignore one of its members. This generally creates intense emotional turmoil in that group member, sometimes hidden behind a mute, withdrawn or angry facade. The method and timeliness in the provision of the needed support to the excluded group member is a matter of judgment and will vary from situation to situation, but if no other group member offers support, the trainer will personally have to model and provide it in order to reduce the stress. Due to the trainer's position of power in the group, other group members are then usually able to rally and also open themselves, at least to some degree, to the rejected group member. (See Case 4 in Chapter 7.) In the less severe distress reactions, when a group member simply appears tense, making eye contact with and smiling or giving an affirmative nod may be all that is needed in assuring a group member that he or she is valued.

Shift the Work Focus

The group was processing the morning session when Mary suddenly started to sob, her whole body shaking. She did not respond when the group leader asked her about what was happening to her and seemingly could

Table 6.1 Do's in Laboratory Education: A Guide for Trainers

I. Before the Program

- Read the application forms before the participants arrive.
- Resist the temptation to bring vulnerable participants into the program even if they come from far away or are "important people."
- Check which participant lives away from the learning community or has brought family along. Check which participant has done several programs in succession.
- Make contact with the clinical consultant (psychiatrist).
- Build a staff team that is in a learning stance so that feedback from other staff is welcome.

II. During the Program

- While training be sure to be available to your group 24 hours a day. This includes the free time.
- Have as many observers present as possible in the opening session.
- Ask participants to monitor their stress levels. Remind them to get enough sleep, exercise, food. Ask them to go easy on alcohol intake.
- Ask participants to inform staff beforehand if they intend to miss a session.
- Decide if you have any high-risk participants in your group and share this information with your staff and the clinical consultant as quickly as possible after the beginning of the event.
- Be sure to restate the goals of the program and stick to them.
- Present a program schedule to the group and stick to it.
- Make personal contact with each participant in your group as quickly as possible.
- Be respectful of the participants' right to stop their work whenever they feel finished.
- Stop any "ganging up" on a participant by the group.
- Interrupt a participant's work if you sense that the stress level is getting too high. Renegotiate the continuance of the work.
- Prevent the participant from working on a deeper level than the particular set of group participants can support.
- If you have a strong negative emotional reaction to any participant's behavior, analyze it within yourself as well as with your team to see if it could be a transference reaction.
- Consult with other staff when you have a strong negative reaction to a participant.
- As much as possible, let other staff handle the group work of any participant toward whom you have a negative transference.
- Have participants communicate to you and the other participants about how they plan to spend their afternoon and evening off.

- Take participants' concerns over the emotional state of another participant seriously.
- When you observe deviant behavior in a participant, give feedback when it occurs. Avoid surprises when you have to give a negative evaluation at the end of the lab.
- Do your best to assure that a vulnerable participant has a safe trip home.

III. After the Program

- Be available to your participants by letter or phone.

IV. Always

- Prevent an incident if possible. It's always easier than managing one.

not respond to touch from two other group members. The processing was put aside and the work shifted to Mary. Although the time for the session was almost over, the group and the trainer worked with Mary until she was able to contract with the group that she would deal with her issues in the next session after lunch.

It turned out that Mary had lost her mother on that very day a year before and that she had been in treatment for depression for the last half-year. In affective learning groups the focus of the work needs to be where the greatest emotional valence resides. Adhering to outlines and schedules is important; rigidity, however, is potentially detrimental.

Although the group leader may be anxious to get back to the "real" work of the group once a psychotic participant is safely hospitalized, the other group members are likely not to be ready to return to it. They may have many questions about the meaning of what they saw in their midst and may require factual information. Additionally they may have to deal with their feelings of impotence, fright, and even guilt. The trainer should not be surprised to learn that some group members feel anger towards her or him either for not having omnipotently prevented the incident or for having abandoned the group to take care of the dysfunctional group member.

Topics need to be changed and schedules need to be altered at times in order to shift the focus from an individual within a group who is significantly upset. It has been our experience that a debriefing session, so to speak, has to be offered to a group after a significant, clinical incident has occurred. Ignoring distress signals, whether they are sent by an individual or by the

Table 6.2 Strategies for Stress Reduction in Small Group Work

- Give support verbally
  - Express interest
  - Express understanding physically
- Shift focus of work
  - To a different person
  - To a different level
    - Group
    - versus interpersonal
    - versus individual
  - To a different mode
    - Process versus content
    - Thought versus emotion
- Enforce healthy group norms
  - Psychological safety
  - Physical safety
- Model appreciation of differences
- Model nondefensiveness
- Offer alternative perspective
  - Encourage positive self-talk
  - Reframe "deviant" behavior

group as a whole, is likely to lead to clinical incidents or worsen the intensity and impact of an incident in progress. We believe that ignoring a group's request for a debriefing session is probably one of the reasons why additional clinical incidents are not uncommon in groups in which a major one has already occurred.

Shifting the focus of the program's work to a different level may also reduce stress. The control stage of group work is the stage that many group members find most stressful. Attacks by group members on the trainer or the struggle for leadership among group members is stimulating and energizing to some personality types. Others, however, find it uncomfortable at best, frightening at worst. Group tension can become so intense that it is almost palpable. Shifting focus from the interpersonal struggle to a discussion of "What is happening with our group right now?" can shift the level and mode of the group work. Group members may experience that shift as a tremendous relief. It is almost like opening a safety valve when group members learn that their power struggles are not only predictable but also a necessary and normal part of group development. An example of shifting the focus from emotion to thought, and how that type of intervention can reduce stress, is illustrated by Case 3 in Chapter 7, when Margie focuses James's attention on the "here and now" rather then allowing him to withdraw into his emotion-laden world of psychotic reality.

Enforce Healthy Group Norms

At times, groups can put an enormous amount of pressure on their members to conform to simple things like seating arrangements or a style of dress, language, depth of self disclosure, or the amount of emotion expressed. The trainer has to be aware of such pressure and the potentially adverse influence it can have on some group members. He or she may have to ask a group member with a back condition, who is being pressured to sit with the group in a circle on the floor rather than in a chair, "Joe, is that really okay for your back?" The trainer may also have to remind a group member that he or she is in charge of the amount and depth of the work he chooses to do, and that it is okay to stop for a while. It is not unusual for novice group members to want to stop their work because of the high intensity of feelings generated yet not know how to extricate themselves from it without the trainer's intervention.

Another important guideline for the management of a distress reaction is to keep the participant and the group physically safe. Safety becomes an issue during more severe distress reactions. A participant with suicidal thoughts needs to be under constant observation until mental health professionals can take over his or her care. An incoherent participant may be too preoccupied with his or her internal processes to, for example, negotiate highway traffic safely, or to safely drive a car. Severely disturbed participants must not be sent home on a bus without accompaniment, and cannot be trusted to negotiate the complexities of airline travel. Also, an angry participant must not be allowed to terrorize the group verbally or physically. *Physical violence of any kind cannot be permitted and must be stopped as soon as it occurs.*

Of course, group leaders cannot by themselves create a climate that is conducive to inquiry and emotional openness. Much depends on the group's composition. But if trainers do not stop verbal or physical abuse as soon as it arises, the group cannot flourish, and constructive learning is not possible. What is considered verbal abuse is open to interpretation. In some settings, name calling constitutes verbal abuse while in others it may only be considered an ineffective way of making a point. The trainer will need to be sensitive to the setting and type of people in the group, and not use his or her own tolerance level as the sole guide of what is an appropriate group norm. This is especially important for trainers involved in multicultural work.

Sometimes, skillful immediate intervention on an individual level, as in the following case, can turn a potentially explosive situation into a meaningful, affection-building experience for both the individual and the group. Paul frightened his T-group when he responded to Karen's angry remarks about how he was conducting himself in the group by saying that he would like to break her neck because she was hurting and torturing him, "just like my mother did." The group became silent and one could sense the rising tension in the room. All eyes went to the trainer as he stood and placed himself physically beside Paul and touched him lightly. He eased the tension by saying to Paul, "You got in touch with a lot of rage just now, Paul. Apparently much of that anger has its roots in your childhood. Karen was just a lightning rod for it." Paul thought for awhile and then nodded.

For the next several minutes the trainer worked with Paul, allowing him to experience the rage within himself, and to become aware of the underlying fear and pain of rejection that fueled this rage. Slowly, Paul was able to talk about the deep hurt he had experienced because of his mother's abuse. The group was genuinely moved, and some members were able to respond by holding Paul as he sobbed. Later on, Paul was able to listen as group members confronted Karen's blaming and critical style in a way that was not inflammatory. The nonverbal component of this intervention may have contributed significantly to the successful outcome. Shadish (1980) discusses the apparent positive effect of nonverbal interventions on group cohesion.

The trainer's physical move to sit right beside Paul (a structural intervention) gave three messages to the group and to Paul: (a) that he felt competent to deal with Paul's anger, (b) that Paul could be trusted not to become violent, and (c) that Paul very much needed support. This trainer's immediate and skillful attention to Paul helped the group understand

Paul's anger and violent feelings with the result that the group became cohesive, and Paul remained a fully included member.

On rare occasions psychotic people do become violent. This occurs mostly when they feel cornered or trapped. Should a trainer choose to be alone in a room with a potentially violent person, it is good practice that he or she be positioned closest to the door and that it is kept ajar. Using this precaution, what goes on in the room can be monitored by others outside the room and the trainer can feel the effects of a safety net if anything dangerous should occur. A paranoid participant will need a great deal of control over his environment and may not want anyone to ask probing questions, come too close physically, or tell him what to do. Touching a paranoid person is not prudent and, although well meant, may be experienced by the paranoid person as an intrusion. On the other hand, the disorganized, incoherent participant will do better when structure is imposed. He may actually calm down when being reassured that people are there for him and though they will not "crowd" him they also will not desert him. Generally, providing a comfortable environment for the psychotic participant goes a long way in alleviating agitation.

While the trainer is waiting for a mental health professional to arrive, he or she does not need to be afraid of talking to and/or dealing with a disorganized or incoherent participant. No special skills other than compassion and empathy are necessary to care for a psychotic participant. The task is simple: Be there to reassure, and if needed, to watch for his safety.

Model Appreciation of Differences

Trainers are ill-equipped to work in groups if they have not taken time to grapple with their own inherent sexism and racism. Both appear to be part of the human condition. To recognize them within ourselves in their often subtle shapes will allow us to recognize their effect in groups (Case 1 in Chapter 7 is an example of gross gender bias and of racism). A trainer's tendency to nod to remarks only by group members of the same gender or race is a subtle one. This subtle clue to bias may be picked up unconsciously or consciously by group members who are different and give them vague discomfort. When a trainer sees discrimination of significant proportion, just modeling appreciation of the other may provide enough stress relief in the devalued group member to make a difference. At other times, more formal attention to the issues through education or through formation of same gender or race groups, may be needed to decrease tension and distress.

Model Nondefensiveness

At times, trainers will make mistakes that contribute to an escalation of anxiety or anger in a group member. To acknowledge that one should have intervened earlier or clarified a group norm earlier, may help decrease the person's distress. This may be done in private. More often it is useful for the entire group to hear the acknowledgement; although, it may create discomfort in some who still need to perceive the leader as infallible and omniscient. Acknowledging one's mistake models nondefensiveness, and brings out the trainer's willingness to be a learner too, which in turn may move the group closer to accomplishing its tasks competently, instead of looking to the trainer for all the answers.

Offer Alternative Perspectives

As discussed in Chapter 2, distress is a psychological as well as a physical response to the impact of behaviors and words in groups. However, it is not the events or the words themselves that produce distress. They represent the stimuli. Different people respond to the same event or words with emotions varying in intensity and quality from neutral, to excitement, to distress. The way in which we interpret events or words within ourselves determines our emotional response. Keeping this chain of events in mind gives the trainer a great opportunity to help decrease a participant's stress level. By inquiring "What does it mean to you that Jason criticized you?" the trainer may hear answers like, "Men never like me" or "He sounded just like my father" or "I can't do anything right." Depending on the type of group in which the incident occurred, the trainer may facilitate positive feedback by other group members (an interpersonal level of intervention) or may have the group member say aloud things she has done right, in order to help her recognize the falsehood of her over-generalizing self-talk (an individual level of intervention).

Relabeling is closely related to changing negative self-talk. (Case 3 in Chapter 7 is an example of how the group leader relabeled James' psychotic break a "stress reaction," which made it something familiar to everyone in the room, and effectively removed its stigma.) Relabeling is often immediately effective in reducing stress levels. *Rational-Emotive therapy* and *cognitive psychotherapy* are systems built on changing emotional reactions through cognitive, rational examination of negative self-talk. Although laboratory education is not therapy, an understanding of how common negative self-talk is changed in those therapies is useful for group leaders. The reader who wants to familiarize him- or herself more with those ideas is referred to the work of Beck, Rush, Shaw, and Emery (1979); Burns (1980); Ellis and Harper (1975).

The Role of Peer and Psychiatrist Consultation

Distress reactions in participants frequently raise stress levels in trainers, diluting their ability to examine all intervention options and choose appropriate ones. A trainer is not being fair to him- or herself when he or she neglects to talk over his observations and concerns with another knowledgeable person. Peer consultation can be an invaluable tool for managing distress safely and effectively. Consultation is most effective when it is put into place before the problems have reached clinical proportions, but, the old saying "better late than never" applies here also. Together with a supportive peer, a trainer can better map out an appropriate course of action. This approach has its counterpart in theories of administration that advocate participatory management in order to provide insurance against leader and organizational regression (Kernberg, 1978a, 1978b).

When the group leader is fortunate enough to have a co-leader available, he or she will be able to compare notes with someone else who has firsthand knowledge of the incident. Even though the co-leader may be a trainee, important insights may arise simply by comparing mental notes.

Groups are complex structures, with many different levels of events occurring simultaneously. The group leader is hard pressed to monitor them all. Based on our experience it is wise to use co-leaders whenever affective groups are run for mental health trainees or professionals, especially in the rare but potentially high-risk situation in which the group leader and participants have an ongoing formal relationship.

It is unfortunate that economic realities prohibit the routine use of co-leaders in experiential learning groups. This makes it tougher to get on-the-spot peer consultation. Some group leaders, however, have found value in voluntary collaboration groups to allow regular debriefing of the difficult cases in their practice. Others have set up an informal network of friends who are professionals in the field and who can be contacted when problems arise.

In Chapter 5 we discussed the importance of having a psychiatrist available for backup whenever groups are run that focus on affective learning. When peer consultation is not available or when different expertise may be needed, the trainer will then have the option to consult the psychiatrist. If and when to consult the psychiatrist on call can be a difficult question for the group leader. Often the answer is obvious: In cases of severe disturbance (i.e., severe depression, panic, or psychosis) the psychiatrist consultant should be contacted as quickly as possible. If the psychiatrist is not readily available, the dysfunctional participant should be taken to the nearest hospital emergency room for a psychiatric evaluation. On the other end of the spectrum, many trainers, especially the clinically experienced ones, feel comfortable handling brief anxiety or depressive reactions without psychiatric input.

Many other distress reactions fall between these extremes. They need to be decided on an individual basis. As a general rule, psychiatric consultation should be elicited whenever the trainer finds him- or herself so preoccupied with a distressed participant that he or she cannot adequately track the remainder of the group. Similarly, if the trainer finds it necessary to engage in more than one lengthy conversation with the participant outside of the group, it is time to involve a consultant.

In Bethel, Maine, NTL staffs have psychiatrist consultants available who have made a special effort to become familiar with laboratory education and the values/norms of a learning community. They are consulted frequently, usually early in a problem's development, and usually quite effectively. Other environments may require more trainer effort to obtain a consultation, but the investment of energy is necessary and worthwhile. As mentioned in Chapter 4, it is advisable to establish a relationship with a psychiatrist consultant during the pregroup planning phase. The preprogram contact can clarify the roles and expectations of both the training staff and the consultant. Optimally the trainers and consultants will be familiar and comfortable with one another before a crisis occurs. The crisis itself is not a good relationship builder because of the stress and anxiety for all. Unfortunately, all too often the on-call consultant is never contacted except when a crisis occurs. When seeking psychiatric consultation it may help to remember that most good clinical practitioners themselves seek peer consultation frequently for their more difficult problems. They value the experience positively and do not see it as a sign of incompetence or lack of skill.

It is a mark of professionalism if the organizers of a learning event anticipate the need for crisis intervention and provide for the availability of a psychiatrist consultant. There is often debate over the appropriateness of specifying a psychiatrist as compared to a psychologist, psychiatric social worker, or other clinician. The disciplines of the authors of this book include psychiatry and psychology, and we agree upon the added value of using a psychiatrist as the consultant. A psychiatrist consultant can be a more effective triage person, especially since the appropriate intervention may, at times, require medication or even hospitalization. In addition insurance issues often tend to favor the use of a qualified psychiatrist.

Neither psychology nor psychiatry clinical training programs equip the practitioner to understand laboratory education. Both the choice and education of a consultant who can "fit" the applied arenas of experiential learning are necessary. Practitioners who are unfamiliar with the technology and principles of experiential learning may undervalue, indeed be critical of, its value and effectiveness. Such a practitioner may also be more inclined to deal with situations out of context and take a purely clinical approach to a problem.

The psychiatrist consultant is of value in two roles. The psychiatrist's primary role is that of consultant to the group leader or trainer of an event. To the degree possible, it is preferable to keep a distressed participant in the program so that the participant, the other members of the group, and the trainer all experience the success of completing the program. This is especially so if one accepts that stress per se is not a sufficient reason to abandon the learning effort but is indeed part of the process. Therefore, the psychiatrist's first attempt is to consult with the trainer and provide guidance on what the trainer can do to manage the situation. The consultant who views his or her primary role as providing preventative consultation will probably be both more effective and better received by the training staff.

This is not always easy to do because the trainer is often anxious about the situation and may, as explained in Chapter 3, be experiencing some counter-transference with negative feelings about the participant. The trainer may be applying subtle or not so subtle pressure on the consultant to get the "difficult person" out of his group, or he may want to hand "the problem" over to the psychiatrist. At such times, the consultant must decide if the trainer is able to use consultation to find ways to see the participant with empathy, to manage his own feelings and to manage the difficult participant. Consultants who do not go along with a group leader's negative perception of a participant may be viewed by a trainer as unresponsive, uncaring, or in other ways not performing the consultant role properly.

The laboratory education culture can also be a barrier to using the consultant in the clinical intervention role. An example from our experience is an instance in which the trainer accompanied a distressed participant to the psychiatrist and objected to the "distancing effect" of the consultant's insistence on being addressed as "Doctor." Informality and intimacy are often norms in experiential learning, and the trainer assumed that this would be true when using a consultant. The participant was experiencing a brief acute psychotic episode and establishing boundaries was an important part of the clinical intervention. Not knowing this, the trainer created distrust of the consultant on the part of the participant and set up complicating dynamics during the introduction of the clinical consultant.

There is a final point to be made about the use of a psychiatrist consultant. The trainer, or group leader, may find that no matter how much he or she would like to seek assistance, the trainer's self-esteem or sense of professional competence is threatened. In spite of his or her own discomfort the trainer needs to keep the best interest of the participants in mind and use the appropriate resources.

Certainly there is a clinical intervention role for the consultant even if it is viewed as a secondary role. In this case it is essential to have a competent clinician available. The psychiatrist consultant may have direct contact with the distressed participant in order to assess if there is a psychiatric illness underneath the distress reaction exhibited and how severe it might be. Usually the consultant needs to see the distressed group member no more than once. The majority of clinical incidents will be acute episodes of short duration, often caused by lack of sleep or substance abuse. Generally psychiatrist consultants to laboratory education events prefer to talk the participant down rather than use medication.

Historically, other approaches have been tried. Evaluating these options has led us to believe that, if medication is necessary to relieve stress or to stabilize a participant's behavior, it must be used *only as a last resort*. A recently medicated participant may not be in a position to benefit further from the learning group environment. Hospitalization is rare, indeed. In the collective experience of the authors, serious episodes have only occurred with persons who had a preexisting condition. Most often, consultation with training staff and direct intervention with participants result in successful completion of the program.

Whether to retain responsibility or to pass it on to the psychiatrist consultant can be a confusing dilemma for the trainer. Once resorting to the use of a consultant in the clinical role, letting go and cooperating with the consultant's intervention is the goal.

The psychiatrist consultant will want or need certain information. Collecting this data prior to the consultation will greatly facilitate the process. Table 6.3 presents a list of the information the consultant will need to know in order to provide a valid consultation.

We recommend that the trainer and consultant plan the strategies for the next intervention together. Many interventions can be created during a consultation session. The success of these alternative measures is in proportion to the degree of openness with which the session is conducted. In general, interventions that work to maintain a participant's membership in the learning group are those designed contextually, thoughtfully, and with the individual and group's needs and strengths in mind. The stage of

Table 6.3 Useful Information for the Consulting Psychiatrist

- Type of group and brief summary of the learning goals
- Current stage of group development (Schutz)
- Participant's differences in regard to age, gender, color, education, culture or other as compared to majority
- Participant's specific behaviors which have aroused concern
- Group's reaction to the incident
- Participant's history of previous emotional distress; history of psychotherapy or psychiatric hospitalization
- Participant's history of specific life stresses; recent transitions, losses
- Participant's learning goals
- Participant's role in the group
- Participant's known support system in the laboratory and back home
- Any current physical illness or complaints
- Any sleep or appetite disturbances
- Suspected or known alcohol or drug use
- Any current medication use (exact name, dose, how often)

---

the group's development, the comfort level and skill of the trainer and the available support system for the participant must also be considered.

There are times when the intensity of a participant's distress reaction is so great that being part of the group is too stressful and the amount of time spent in the group must be adjusted. This is obviously a high intensity intervention with broad implications. We strongly recommend therefore that the clinical consultant be involved in this decision. There are a variety of options to consider. The group member might be encouraged to participate only in community sessions, or small work groups, but not in the more emotionally stressful groups. He or she might silently participate in all parts of the program for a day or so, as if auditing it, with careful debriefing by the trainer intermittently. He or she could skip half a day of sessions to get some rest, then try returning to a full schedule, or he or she may actually be helped to leave the program early.

Two considerations must be weighed. On the one hand, it is generally counterproductive to try keeping a severely distressed group member in the group if that member, or the group, cannot continue to learn because of the distress reaction. On the other hand, experience has shown that it is best overall if a group member can complete the program in spite of having had a distress reaction. Having to leave prematurely usually generates feelings of inadequacy and failure that may intensify after the return home. This may be avoided if an incident is dealt with in an understanding and caring manner within the learning community. Also, learning incurred from a distress reaction is often an extremely powerful inducer of insight or change, not only for the individual who had the distress reaction but also for other group members. Though a hard way to learn, in retrospect such experiences can be pivotal in a person's life.

It is not surprising, therefore, that different trainers will have different opinions as to whether a distressed participant should leave a program early. That conflict, of course, requires extensive discussion among the staff. The staff's various opinions deserve to be examined in depth, in order to arrive at a well thought out, joint decision. The final decision, except in the most severe cases of dysfunction, is best arrived at as a joint decision between participant and staff.

Based on our experience, there are definite indications when a distressed participant should be helped to leave the group early. They are summarized in Table 6.4.

Being advised to leave is sometimes a great emotional relief. This is especially so for the participant who has difficulty extracting him- or herself from a situation that is too stressful, for fear of being seen as a quitter or as someone without backbone.

When a decision is reached to continue with the program but on a limited schedule, careful monitoring of the participant is important. His or her progress should be checked regularly to make certain there is no recurrence of the dysfunction or a worsening of the problem. Is he attending the sessions? Is he able to cope with the stress of the group process? Is he integrated into the social activities of the group during free time? Are his appetite and sleep normal? If distress continues to be present or if significant dysfunction in any of the above areas lingers or worsens, the staff can then decide on different interventions and implement them.

Table 6.4 Reasons to Facilitate Early Departure

- The participant is a danger to himself or others.
- The participant has a condition which requires major tranquilizers or antidepressants.
- The participant wants to return to the support of his family or therapist.
- The participant develops a distress reaction because his learning goals did not match the learning goals of the group.

The Termination Phase and Follow-Up

As mentioned above, group members whose behavior has deviated markedly from the group norm, whether they finish the group or leave early, frequently feel a sense of shame that they "fell apart," "went crazy," or "lost it." They see themselves as more vulnerable than the rest of the group, as defective. Real relief can be offered by other group members or trainers who tell them about similar episodes in their own lives, or in their family's lives, when high stress temporarily broke through their usual coping mechanisms. Those kind of reports normalize the distress reaction for the participant and may draw attention to the importance of monitoring his or her own general stress level. Although other participants may not identify with some of the more severe reactions, it is nevertheless extremely important that the distressed participant has a chance to talk over his or her feelings about the incident. Should the participant recover sufficiently to stay throughout the session, the consultant, the trainer, or group members will want to set aside time to help the participant understand his distress reaction and to develop strategies for managing excessive stress more effectively in the future.

When a trainer has appropriately managed the environment and performed according to a program's contract, most participants will have a positive group learning experience. No follow-up is needed. Participants tell each other and their group leader that they will stay in touch but rarely do so for any length of time, even though the experience may have been an emotionally intense and useful one. However two types of group members may require follow-up contact after the event has ended: (a) those who leave a group before its conclusion, and (b) those who complete the program but have experienced high stress or distress during the course of the laboratory. It has been our experience that it is best for the group leader and/or the sponsoring institution to stay involved with those two kinds of participants beyond the end of the group. The involvement does not have to continue for long but needs to be there long enough to ensure that the participant is indeed stable. In those cases in which the instability persists, involvement can be terminated once the participant has been successfully transferred to the care of his or her family or an appropriate professional.

Even if a participant leaves the group for reasons apparently unrelated to psychological distress (e.g., back home emergencies or medical problems), follow-up is highly recommended. Certainly, any participant who leaves a program in a distressed state requires follow-up. Remaining with the group until the program is over is not necessarily evidence that the distress was coped with adequately and that clinical repercussions will not occur once the participant returns home. Unfortunately, as alluded to in Chapter 4 (Yalom & Lieberman, 1971), peer judgment, *not* trainer judgment, is often more accurate in predicting "who got hurt" in the group and who may, therefore, have significant postgroup distress. It stands to reason that some distressed participants may, therefore, not get the follow-up they deserve, simply because the group leader does not know about their problems. The field of experiential group work has matured since that study was made. However, the data stands as a warning to all trainers to be very careful—that is, full of care. Some group leaders have made it a practice to give out their phone number at the conclusion of a group event to provide a safety net for any unrecognized post group "casualties."

Finally, the importance of detailed documentation of all clinical incidents cannot be overemphasized. It is best to write an incident report not only on those participants known to have experienced distress reactions during a program but also on any participant who missed, with a vague excuse, one or more sessions. Also, participants who leave early for any reason deserve the documentation of an incident report.

The need for documentation in today's litigious society is apparent to anyone working in business, medicine, or mental health. It is absolutely necessary to track high-risk or distressed participants in a way that captures the salient features of the incident and that provides a solid description and chronology of the interventions, both during and after the laboratory.

Considering the variety of clinical incidents that occur in groups, it is not possible to develop a single follow-up procedure that would be appropriate for all the different incidents encountered. Design of an individual follow-up plan for participants who have suffered distress reactions, therefore, is the task of the staff team. Their follow-up plan should be formulated before they leave the site and must be very specific: What type of follow-up is recommended? Who is to do it? What is the timing? See Table 6.5 for suggested steps following a clinical incident.

The level of follow-up intensity depends on a number of variables, such as the degree of distress or dysfunction the participant suffers upon leaving the program, the strength of the support system to which the participant returns, the participant's past ability (or inability) to cope with high stress, the length of time and complexity of travel involved in returning the participant to his or her support system, and the availability of staff for support once the event is over. The most severe clinical incidents will obviously require the most detailed documentation of progress and interventions. The trainer and the sponsoring institution must collaborate closely.

Participants who experience distress at the end of a program may be the most difficult for trainers to handle. This usually is a stressful time for staff also because of the many demands on their time and energy. Making a transition from work to home or to another job, completing paperwork, parting from participants and colleagues, and meeting travel schedules may mean the staff is emotionally less available to a distressed participant. However, responsible training means allowing extra time at this critical phase in the life of a group. Trainers should be available to detect and deal with any participant whose stress level appears to be too high. Therefore, careful trainers will not schedule their departures or subsequent work assignments too close to the final session.

As mentioned above, whenever a distressed participant leaves a group, whether it be prior to the end of the group or at the conclusion of the group, care needs to be taken to make the journey home a safe one. Depending on the severity of the dysfunction, the trainer may have to contact family or professionals in the participant's home town and inform them about the

Table 6.5 Suggested Steps Following a Clinical Incident

- Document the incident in detail and accurately. If there are different perspectives be sure to have others document also.
- Process the incident with your staff.
- Decide on a follow-up plan for the distressed participant and stick to it.
- Steer the group to openly express any feelings which arose because of the incident, should the group not do so on its own.
- If the distressed participant has a therapist, get permission from the participant to contact that therapist.
- Look at yourself honestly to see if anything in your attitude or behavior increased the distress of the participant or failed to decrease it.
- When a transference reaction on your part contributed to the problem, let future work staffs know about your vulnerability in that area.
- When a transference reaction on your part contributed to the problem, consider further self-understanding, e.g., psychotherapy for yourself.

incident. Of course, unless an emergency exists, such contact should never be made without the *explicit consent of the participant.*

Fortunately, most distressed participants do not require this extreme level of follow-up care. More common strategies are a follow-up call or two from trainer to participant, or vice versa, a few days after the program to monitor the participant's stress level. A mild depression within a week following the return home is such a common occurrence that it may be considered normal. For an already marginally coping group member, however, the postgroup letdown can be serious. Trainers will want to be sure that their charge traversed this critical time period safely.

Braaten (1979) described a number of dilemmas in group training. The follow-up of clinical incidents has its own dilemma. One principle of laboratory education is that the participant is not only encouraged but indeed expected to be responsible for him- or herself and his or her own learning. Once a clinical incident has been identified, the trainer temporarily takes over various degrees of responsibility for the sake of the participant's well-being. This can be an uncomfortable role both for the trainer and the participant. The most successful follow-up is one that returns to the participant the responsibility to manage his or her affairs as soon as possible (i.e., let the participant initiate that phone call to solicit support), yet provides comprehensive, active support as long as the participant is in acute distress.

Trainers in laboratory education meet a large number of people and touch many lives significantly. Even though most participants in laboratory education will be able to manage their learning without distress, those who experience distress can, with the help of competent staff, frequently turn crisis into an opportunity for growth. Trainers must live the norms they support in programs. When the participant experiences honest and empathic understanding from the staff, and feels a staff member's willingness to be there for however long it takes to traverse the acute crisis, he or she knows that the experience was genuine.

Conclusion

The more severe a distress reaction is, the more a trainer's interventions will have to focus on the individual rather than on a group level. Containing a distress reaction to prevent further escalation, obtaining consultation regarding its management, providing a safe environment for the afflicted participant and the group, joint decision making in regard to the group member's level of further participation in the group, and normalization of the participant's perception of his distress reaction are the main objectives of the management of distress. The importance of follow-up and documentation of the incident and its management cannot be overemphasized.

7. CASE STUDIES

From time to time, high-intensity clinical incidents will occur in small group work. In spite of the group leader's best efforts, not all of them can be prevented. To assist participants and trainers alike in thinking through effective interventions, the following ten cases of threatening experiences in groups have been created. Names and details of the incidents are fictional. The types of incidents described, however, are representative of the types of incidents consultants encounter in small group work.

The cases were chosen to represent examples of the four quadrants of the Johari Window of Distress Reactions (see Chapter 3) and hopefully will give the reader a broader understanding of the presentation and management of major clinical incidents in groups. Although management strategies were offered, it should be apparent from what has been stated earlier in this manual that different strategies could have been chosen, especially if the setting or the type of group had been different.

Case 1

"I am sick and tired of this," shouted Robert as he stood up and pointed a finger at Barbara. "Nobody can tell me whether to talk or when to talk.

95

Certainly not you, black bitch. You think you know what is going on in my mind, you think you know how I should be leading my life. Well, nobody can tell me how to act in this group. You are not the leader here, although you obviously would like to be. I am not taking orders from women. I am not staying in this group. This group is a waste of time." With the words "Who needs this?" Robert walked toward the door. The group sat in stunned silence.

Direct attacks on a group member or the trainer occur commonly in small group work. They require immediate and decisive interventions in order to prevent psychological harm. Attacks are especially vicious and toxic in their effect on the group when a personal attack is combined with a stereotypical statement, for example Robert's reference to Barbara's race. An attack of that type almost guarantees that not only will the person who was attacked become upset but also other group members in the room will feel attacked, or else feel compelled to protect the attacked person.

Robert had used the first two sessions of this T-group for corporate managers to talk excessively about his work, his style of running a company division, his socializing with important people, and how he thought this group should be run. The group had difficulty coalescing because of Robert's domineering style. Barbara, therefore, had asked him to please be quiet for a little while and give other group members who had not had a chance to say something about themselves to be heard. Although the intensity of Robert's outburst was unusually high, conflict between group members is an integral part of all small group work and may in fact be grist for the mill. Conflict is part of the human condition. With skillful intervention and as long as the group members in conflict have sufficient emotional resilience, much learning can come out of dealing positively with conflict in groups.

Leaving a group is the most common incident that occurs following a crisis in small group work. Occasionally it is even recommended to a participant by the trainer (see Chapter 6). Nevertheless, the group member who can be persuaded not to leave until after the conflict has been worked out, or at least contained, generally fares better in the long run than someone who leaves impulsively when an interpersonal problem erupts. Obviously, it is also of greater benefit for the group as a whole if its members can express their feelings of anger, guilt, hopelessness, and helplessness directly to the participant who evoked them. Sometimes there is actually a turnaround and the upset individual becomes an included, appropriate group member. When the aim of the attack, however, is broad (for example in Robert's case it was against Barbara as a person, not just at a behavior of hers and also against women and blacks in general), the group's work is often hindered significantly and therefore eventual exclusion of the person may be inevitable. It is, however, important that some type of positive closure is accomplished around the incident. "He's just a prejudiced, controlling white male who was probably sent by his company to get 'fixed'"; "He would have just slowed the group down"; "So glad he showed his true colors early and decided to leave," are poor trainer responses to Robert's anger, even if not said out loud.

When there is just one trainer in the group, which is unfortunately the usual situation, he or she can stay on top of conflict better if the upset individual remains with the group. Therefore, one of the first things a trainer should do is engage an upset participant like Robert enough so that he can stay in the room. The exception is a participant who threatens violence; physical distance would then, in fact, be advantageous. To keep an enraged participant in the room could actually fuel emotional turmoil and may lead to a dangerous lack of control.

Ideally, intervention to keep the participant in the room would come from another group member. However, if the group is too overwhelmed or unable to muster the empathy needed to deal with a group member whose value system is different from their own, then it is the responsibility of the trainer to deal directly with the participant who threatened to leave. There are several methods. The trainer can try to persuade the participant to stay by finding something positive in the derogatory statements the participant made. After all, in the example above, Robert finally expressed his feelings rather than continuing to talk about his importance in his life back home. Such an interaction constitutes an individual intervention. However, a process comment also could be made, such as, "Robert, you helped us come to an important point in this group. You brought us to the point where we have to deal with conflict (a conceptual, individual/group, medium intensity intervention). Conflict resolution is one of the toughest things, both in our personal lives as well as in organizations. The conflict that you have raised here can help all of us become more aware of our favorite ways of dealing with conflict and see how useful they really are to us. It might give us a chance to experiment with different ways. Good results can come out of this."

If the upset group member does not respond to a few attempts to keep him in the room, another way of dealing with an individual like Robert would be for the trainer to let Robert know that he or she will be available to talk with him after the group, or at the next meal (a structural, individual, low-intensity intervention). Unless the group member appears to be a threat to him- or herself or to others, it is generally not necessary for the trainer to stop the session and pursue the distressed participant. Whenever a trainer is uneasy about an upset group member being alone outside of the group's view, another participant could be asked to follow him. This intervention is especially useful when there is someone in the group who has good rapport with the member in crisis.

Using the Johari Window of Distress Reaction, Robert's outburst fell into the blind distress reaction quadrant (namely, Quadrant II). Robert was emotionally blind. He had no insight into how inappropriately he was expressing his anger, yet every other person in the room was aware that his behavior was far outside the norm of constructive group behavior. Individuals like Robert are difficult to have in a group because it is likely they will remain blind to their problems out of fear of being controlled by others. They are exceedingly sensitive to criticism and may pick out any small amount of negative feedback that is given, even when it is delivered in carefully measured doses and accompanied with genuine support. The trainer is wise to divert excessive criticism of individuals like Robert, yet still permit the group to let Robert know that name calling, shouting, racial insults, and derogatory statements about women make it difficult to honor Robert's request that they not tell him what to do.

Unless Robert is in a therapy group or personal growth group, it would be counterproductive to try working out his excessive fear of being controlled, or delve into the origins of that fear. That kind of work can only occur if the participant develops some insight into his behavior, namely that he so very much wants to be accepted and admired by others, yet sabotages that completely with his verbal abuse of others. In groups, other than therapy or personal growth groups, the best result a trainer can hope to achieve with a "difficult person" is for that person to consider the possibility that, to an important degree, his own behavior creates his relationship problems. When a difficult person begins to understand that it is not everyone else he comes in contact with who is at fault, as he erroneously assumes, then there may be help for him through long-term, individual psychotherapy to change his attitude and behavior.

Generally, when an incident like the one described occurs in a group, the anxiety level of the group is raised significantly; therefore, unless the trainer deals with the group effectively, further incidents are likely to occur. This is especially true if the distressed participant actually leaves the group. Adequate time must be allotted to allow all group members to process their emotional responses.

In this case, Barbara felt more confused than angry. She needed to know how other group members had interpreted her words to Robert. She had not intended to come across as controlling or critical. She simply wanted to create some air time for a friend of hers who was also in the group and had been very quiet, and for another person who had not yet revealed much about himself. Barbara's friend, Torraine (also a black woman) had become very incensed by Robert's attack on Barbara. It reminded her of her experiences as a young girl in the South, when she had witnessed much abuse of her black mother by white men. With a little encouragement she described the abuse in detail and how helpless and angry she had felt. The group was very moved by her story. Unfortunately, Robert did not hear what Torraine was saying. He had left the group after promising to meet with the trainer over lunch.

The particular group in which the incident occurred was part of a larger basic lab, and two other groups were running concurrently. When the three group trainers discussed the incident, they reported that minority issues were also beginning to surface in their groups. They therefore decided to address the issues immediately and directly. The design was changed. On successive afternoons the entire learning community was divided into two groups—first by race (people of color and whites) and on the second afternoon by gender (a structural, interpersonal, low-intensity intervention). Within the same race, same gender groups, participants discussed how they saw themselves and how they thought they were seen, either by the other race or the other gender. The groups then brought their lists into a combined group session in which with much laughter, comparisons were made and questions were exchanged. The groups continued to meet, of course, on their two-to-three-sessions-a-day schedule and the program closed after six days without further incident.

By the time Robert and his trainer got together over lunch, Robert had calmed down considerably. In fact, he even apologized for losing his temper. After talking over his options and preferences with the trainer, they both concluded it would be good for Robert to join his group briefly after lunch, to let them know he was leaving (a structural, individual, medium intensity intervention). Robert told the group that he needed to reduce his stress to keep from losing his temper, and thought that he could do that better by using the remaining days of his time-off from work on a golf course near his hometown, rather than in a group. The goodbye to the group was cordial enough. When the trainer spoke with Robert on the phone after the conclusion of the lab, Robert sounded fine and inquired how things had gone for his fellow group members.

Case 2

Psychotic incidents rarely occur in groups, but when they do, they usually frighten the group. Many people have not encountered a psychotic person and feel inadequate to deal with them. Psychosis, which means being out of touch with reality, can be subtle and hardly noticeable or it can be blatantly obvious as when Edward, a group member, came to his session with a pillow stuffed into his pants and declared that he was pregnant. There is also no doubt that a person is psychotic when he announces that he is an alien from Mars in disguise as a human. Psychosis may present as grandiose fantasies (delusions) when someone announces that he or she has special powers to heal or harm others through thoughts or that he or she is invulnerable, a "Chosen One," and therefore can walk in front of moving cars without being hurt.

Paranoid thoughts—some may be convinced that others can read their mind, put thoughts into their mind, wish them ill fortune, and actually bring misfortune upon them—are probably the most common kind of delusions encountered. Delusions are one of the hallmarks of psychosis. They are false beliefs to which a psychotic person will cling even though there is no logical evidence to support those beliefs and even in the face of solid evidence that the beliefs cannot be true. Both types of psychosis, the grandiose type and the paranoid psychosis, may or may not be accompanied by hallucinations in which, for example, a person actually hears voices even though no one is talking, or sees, for example, faces or animals even though none are actually there.

Generally, psychotic people will get angry when their delusions or hallucinations are challenged: They know they are right—their senses and their mind tell them so. Psychosis is, therefore, a blind Quadrant III disorder according to the Johari window. No book on human physiology, no scientific evidence, could have convinced Edward that he would not give birth to a baby soon.

The onset of a psychotic state can be fairly sudden or it can be preceded by a period of confusion, rambling, or significantly depressed or elevated mood. The following is a case of a smoldering psychosis that was not recognized during the course of a program but evolved into a full-blown psychotic state at the airport on the way home.

Returning home from a T-group program, Tina wandered about the airport, unable to get well enough organized to board her flight. Airport security was notified by a ticketing agent and a security officer approached Tina. She could not, or would not get on the plane. Instead she kept making reference to the "mission" she was chosen to carry out. She would not explain the nature of the mission. Finally from identification papers she carried in her purse, her family was contacted. Her husband came to the airport, picked her up, and took her to a hospital where she remained for several weeks, requiring antipsychotic medication.

Tina was a twenty-five year old computer programmer who had worked on her job for only about one year. She presented herself in her group as soft spoken, apologetic, and somewhat self-effacing. She had been attentive in her group but did not initiate much conversation with other group members. Her eyes would frequently fill with tears as she listened to the problems other group members were reporting. When she was approached about her tears, she would not reveal the pains in her life but identified with her fellow group members' pain and said that she really could understand how badly they must have felt.

Because of her apparent sensitivity, the group made special efforts to include her in discussions and encouraged her to contribute, yet would not push her when she said, "I'm not ready to bare my soul," or "I appreciate your interest but I need space to sort things out." On the fourth day of a seven-day program, when a woman began speaking about her relationship with her husband, Tina suddenly began sobbing uncontrollably. The group took notice and physically supported Tina. Tina responded by smiling and hugging several group members in appreciation after she had calmed herself down. "If people at home could just be like this group, life would be so much better," was her comment. She then thanked the group for being understanding and redirected them to the person whose work had been interrupted because of her crying episode.

On the fifth day, Tina apparently wanted to share her difficulties on the job and in her marriage. She could not, however, quite bring herself to do it and would stop herself by saying "That is a there-and-then issue," and "I know we're supposed to be dealing with the here-and-now." Or she would just look up at various group members with a smile and say, "I love you all." When the group went out for dinner on the last evening she joined them but later excused herself by saying she had a number of things to do in order to prepare for her departure. The next day, in the final T-group, she looked drawn and haggard, and explained that she had difficulty sleeping. She was quieter than usual and contributed little as the group struggled with termination issues. Tina was absent for the closing session of the group, but she had not told anyone she would not be there. Neither her trainer nor the other group members anticipated that she would not be present.

Although this case was not frightening within the group, it is nevertheless frightening to observe how easy it is to miss an early psychotic process, especially when it occurs at the very end of a program. At that time group leaders are generally busy wrapping up the paper work that needs to be done and planning for their own departure. Therefore, the careful work that is characteristic of good leadership may not be carried out with the same degree of attention on the last day.

Because he was rushed, the trainer did not check on Tina when she failed to show up for the closing session. If the trainer had made contact with Tina prior to her departure, he might have noticed she was having difficulty packing her belongings. She frequently stopped what she was doing and stared vacantly into space. She could not finish sentences because she was distracted by her own thoughts, delusions, or hallucinations. Tina's inability to talk within the group about her problems, even though she apparently wanted to, should have alerted her group leader to the need for a check-in with her. Perhaps a one-to-one talk with her on the fourth day could have released her tensions enough to prevent the full-blown psychotic episode that occurred later at the airport. A few questions about her mood, sleep, appetite, and possible treatment history would have given the trainer a better understanding of the degree of her dysfunction.

Tina had been intensely depressed for several months. She had a history of psychiatric hospitalization for depression in her teens. For fear of not being accepted into this program, however, which she felt was important for her job, she had not revealed that information on the application form. Perhaps she would have felt free to reveal this information to her trainer had such a one-to-one contact occurred. Also, in such a one-to-one meeting, the trainer might have learned about the very high stress Tina was under. She had a two year old baby, and her marriage was about to break up. These high risk factors combined with Tina's difficulties in the group would have undoubtedly alerted her trainer to get in touch with the psychiatrist consultant for advice.

It is well-known that any group member who has a history of psychiatric hospitalization will be more likely to develop significant emotional distress in a group that deals with personal and interpersonal issues. In the case of a severe mental disorder, like a psychotic reaction, the trainer has one primary responsibility: to get the psychiatrist consultant involved as early as possible (see Chapter 6). It is not the trainer's job to treat the disorder. Early identification and keeping the participant safe, however, are in his or her domain.

The trainer's index of suspicion that there is a severe disorder underway should rise when, in a one-to-one meeting with the distressed participant, he or she finds out that there have been sleep or appetite disturbances. As a matter of fact, Tina had been suffering throughout the program from severe difficulty falling asleep, problems staying asleep, and also waking up much too early in the morning. She generally had eaten her meals with the group in the dining room, but had eaten very sparingly. It was not discovered until her hospitalization that she had experienced a marked appetite decrease and had actually lost twenty pounds during the last two months without meaning to lose weight.

Tina's case is an example of a situation that could have resulted in a lawsuit. The severity of her difficulty had not been recognized, psychiatric consultation had not been obtained, family contact had not been established to alert the family that Tina had a problem, assistance was not offered for the trip home, and because the group leader was not aware of Tina's condition, follow-up contact was also not established. In a litigious society, clinical incidents in laboratory education will inspire lawsuits. However, courts are not likely to find a leader guilty of negligence when appropriate steps have been taken to protect a vulnerable participant. Careful documentation of all interventions and attempts to help the participant in crisis are essential to demonstrate to the family and to the court that all reasonable steps were taken to contain the participant's difficulties.

Trainers need to be aware that most serious psychological difficulties occur between the middle and the end of a group. The wise trainer will allow sufficient time after the closing session to be available to any group member who has experienced distress. The trainer should avoid catching a flight home immediately after the closing of the program.

Case 3

On the fourth day of his first T-group laboratory experience, during an exercise on mind/body connection (a structured experience), James appeared to the trainer to become somewhat anxious and agitated. A thirty-five-year-old middle manager from a manufacturing company, James seemed tense and began to mumble. When after the exercise the trainer spoke to him, James told him, "He's come back," and then as if he had no capacity to hold back he blurted out to the group a long-standing history of sporadic experiences with "an imaginary friend" with whom he carried out long conversations. The group was incredulous and one person even remarked to James, "You must be kidding!" When James just looked off into the distance and mumbled and nodded, it quickly became clear that James was indeed serious. At that point, the tension within the group rose visibly. All eyes were on James who seemed oblivious to the group and continued mumbling. At that point Margie, a motherly woman in her fifties, got up and placed herself in a chair in front of James, who did not seem to be aware of her. She gently put her hands on James's knees and asked James to look at her eyes. She assured James that he could talk to his friend again later, but that right now she would like him to look at her (a structural, individual, low-intensity intervention). After repeating her request a few times, James made eye contact with her and stopped mumbling. Margie told him: "Welcome back James. I meant to tell you earlier that I really admired the moccasins you're wearing this morning. Where did you get them?" James looked at his shoes but did not answer.

Margie asked James to look at her eyes again. He promptly did this. She smiled at him, lifted her left hand into his field of vision, and asked him "How many fingers am I showing you on my left hand?" When James responded correctly she did the same with her right hand. While keeping friendly eye contact with James, she then asked him whether he remembered that they had sat across from each other at dinner the night before. When James nodded affirmatively, she proceeded to ask him whether he noticed that there was something different about her head today. James studied her face for awhile but could not come up with anything. Margie told him that she had lost one of her beautiful dangling, silver and turquoise earrings and that thus she was only wearing one earring today. (James had commented on her earrings the night before.) At that point James appeared to relax more.

Margie engaged James in a little more small talk, then asked how he was feeling (an experiential, individual, low-intensity intervention). James said he was fine but did not like all the attention he was getting. Margie moved her chair next to him and stayed there for a while holding his hand (a structural, individual, low-intensity intervention). James took the opportunity to make eye contact with the trainer and other group members. The trainer nodded to James and then made a few remarks to the group about how stress can bring out dormant feelings and behaviors in people. He invited James to join him at lunch if he felt up to it, and James readily accepted. He also asked James whether there was anything he would like from the group. James initially said that he did not need anything, then changed his mind and asked to spend some time with Margie and another woman whom he had sat beside previously during the lab. Both women told him they would be happy to do so. When the trainer suggested that they might take a walk now, James thought it was a good idea. The three departed.

After they were gone, the trainer announced that Margie was an experienced psychotherapist. This was why he had allowed her to handle James. He also reiterated that he would be spending time with James as soon as possible and seek consultation to see how best to help James. He turned back to the original focus of the session, the mind/body exercise, and asked the group if any other reactions to that exercise had occurred. The group was able to refocus on the task and use the remaining time productively.

At lunchtime, the trainer sat with James. They talked about what had happened to him during the mind/body exercise. James could not give a lot of explanation but reported that he was very uncomfortable with body work. It made him anxious. Apparently he had had only a handful of experiences like this in his adult years although as a child he talked to his imaginary friend often. Having had a few too many beers the night before and not having gotten to bed in time to get eight hours of sleep probably contributed. James agreed to be seen by the consulting psychiatrist in the laboratory community and gave permission for the psychiatrist to talk with his therapist back home. It was the therapist back home who supplied the needed information:

James had been adopted into a loving family. Before that, however, his own mother had severely neglected him and reportedly, in one psychotic episode, had the family dog lick the genitalia of her young son on an ongoing basis. When James was first adopted, he had talked a great deal to his imaginary friend but these episodes subsided as he became comfortable in his caring new family. The problems recurred, however, when James seriously contemplated marrying a woman whom he had been dating for several years.

Once the pieces of the puzzle were put together and after James had been seen by the psychiatrist consultant, James apparently returned to his preprogram functioning and was stable enough to finish out the event. He very much wanted to do this. He was advised to not drink alcohol and to get his usual eight hours of sleep. Also, the trainer and James together decided that he would not participate in any nonverbal exercise during the program (structural, individual, low-intensity intervention). On his return home, James continued with his individual psychotherapy to help him understand and overcome his brief hallucinatory episodes and allow him to have a healthier sexual adjustment.

The group was able to keep James as a valued member, partly because James had recovered so quickly from his brief psychotic experience and partly because the trainer had normalized James's reaction by calling it a stress response.

Margie's immediate grounding maneuvers were totally appropriate because they pulled James gently back to reality through firm eye contact, unobtrusive physical contact, and a soothing voice. James's attention was moved to recent events and his observing mind was called upon. This distracted him sufficiently to let go of the hallucinations. The trainer checked with James informally at least daily outside of the group to make sure that James felt all right.

Case 4

An interpersonal learning group was in its second session when Claude, a sharply dressed, lanky, thirty-two-year-old personnel manager, announced that his lover, with whom he had lived for five years, had just been diagnosed as having AIDS. All eyes were on Claude as he made this disclosure. He sobbed, his body shook with the intensity of pain and he moaned, "Raymond, don't leave me!" There was silence in the group. No one moved to comfort him. Finally, Denise, a young woman who had been seen in the bar with Claude the night before, asked him whether he had been tested for the AIDS virus himself. Did he have the disease also? Claude did not answer immediately but when he had calmed down a little, he told her that he had not been tested yet.

He had always been afraid to find out his antibody status and now, he said, it really made no difference to him whether he had also contracted the virus. There was again silence in the group, this time for an extended period of time. Then another member, Ralph shouted, "My God, Claude, why did you come to this program? You're going to get all of us sick!"

At that point the trainer intervened. He went over to Claude, put his arm around him and let him know that he cared about what was happening to him and to his friend (structural/experiential, individual, low-intensity intervention). The trainer expressed his sense of the catastrophe this disease had created for so many wonderful people. Claude looked at the trainer and said, "If you could just know Raymond! He is truly a wonderful man and I cannot believe that he won't be with me. We'd planned to start our own consulting firm later on this year. We'd planned it for several years but were waiting till we had a sounder financial base. That way we could both quit our jobs and work for our own firm. Raymond used to be so full of energy and enthusiasm, a really dynamic guy. People just loved him." And with these words, Claude started to cry again and said, "If it only could have been me who'd gotten infected instead of him. He's so much better than I am. I'd gladly die if he could live." The group was moved. Some even had tears in their eyes. A few moved closer to Claude, forming a small support circle within the larger circle. Someone spoke about losing his favorite university professor to AIDS, though it had not been called AIDS, but "cancer." The professor's students who were aware of his life-style knew, though, that it was AIDS.

Another group member in the circle around Claude reported that he had a cousin who was HIV positive, and told what turmoil had boiled up in the family over it. "We didn't know whether to invite him to the family reunion! Some wanted to act like they didn't know about it, or like the problem didn't exist, and just go on as usual, while others wanted to treat him like a pariah. It was my older brother, who's a doctor, who finally talked to everyone. My cousin actually did come to the family reunion and we had a really great time together. My cousin is sort of a DJ. He had some of us put on a little skit and man, it was funny."

Three or four group members gave Claude support. However, the rest did not join in. Sensing there might be a problem, the trainer stayed beside Claude and invited others to say how they felt about Claude's disclosure (a structural/experiential, individual, medium intensity intervention). Ralph, who had expressed fear of contagion, took the opportunity immediately and said to Claude, "How could you do this to us? You don't belong here. I don't want to share a bathroom with you, or a shower. I can't use the same dishes you've used. Either you go or I go!"

"I'll leave too," said Claude's roommate who had been quiet until now. The trainer explained that even if Claude actually had AIDS, the only way anyone around him could get infected was either through having unprotected sex with him or through his blood, or anything that had come in contact with his blood, like needles. Others supported what the trainer said, yet it was clear that the fearful ones were not convinced. The trainer finally asked if the group felt it would help to bring a doctor in to speak to them about AIDS. They would be able to ask any questions they might have on their minds (a structural, group, low-intensity intervention). The idea was accepted.

Luckily, that evening, the infectious disease specialist of a large HMO in the city was available to speak to the group, and he presented the latest scientific data. His talk corroborated what the group's trainer had been saying earlier, namely that household members of patients with AIDS remain uninfected and therefore safe, as long as any blood spills are cleaned up with Lysol or with a one-to-ten dilution of bleach. The doctor also reiterated that there was no danger to anyone in the lab including roommates. He agreed with the trainer that it would be good for Claude to remain in the group. It was his experience from working with AIDS patients that one of their greatest burdens, besides living with a terminal illness, is the social isolation into which uninformed family and friends so frequently push them. This forced social isolation is almost as painful to them as dealing with their own premature death.

After the physician departed, the trainer promised the group he would make a safe container available to Claude, and some Lysol, so that Claude could dispose of any blood safely, just in case he might accidentally cut himself, say, while shaving. The group member whose cousin had become HIV positive volunteered to be Claude's roommate, a suggestion that his current roommate welcomed indeed. Later that evening the trainer consulted with the psychiatrist consultant about the incident. The psychiatrist felt it was important that he speak to Claude personally, because of the death wishes Claude had expressed at the time of his disclosure. The psychiatrist also advised the trainer to reiterate that whatever goes on in the group, including Claude's disclosure, must be kept absolutely confidential. Toward the end of the program, the trainer recommended to Claude that he seek psychotherapy on his return home, to help deal with his fear of getting tested, and with being discrete about his own HIV status should he be positive, and, of course, to help him with his grief over the probability of losing Raymond in the near future. Ralph did not leave prematurely, and it turned out that in the final session he was actually able to hug Claude and asked his forgiveness for having been so rejecting. Fortunately, this incident occurred in a group of strangers. Had it occurred in a group comprised of Claude's fellow employees, Claude might have had a tough time of it. Word of his possible HIV infection could have spread like wildfire through the company. Social isolation or shunning might have occurred.

Perhaps this incident could have been avoided if the application form for this program had contained a statement that laboratory education can be stressful and that people who are currently under very high stress would do better to postpone their participation in the lab. It is far better to give tuition credit to someone like Claude (whose life crisis arose less than a week prior to the beginning of the program) than to invite an avoidable clinical incident. Incidents draw a lot of energy from the group and its trainer, and often consume much of a trainer's free time while exhausting him.

Generally, the trainer allows the group process to find its own place as it moves through the various stages. When a clinical incident arises, however, the trainer may need to take a very active managerial role as illustrated in Claude's case. The group was not yet in the affection stage; therefore, the trainer had to take it upon himself to model appropriate behavior for the other group members: this meant that he personally comforted Claude. Also, it was the group's trainer, as the manager, who had to set facts straight about a disease that has been compared to the plague and is thus surrounded by a multitude of myths. In addition, the trainer had to alter the schedule to make room for a lecture on AIDS, and he called in the psychiatrist consultant for himself and Claude. The managerial skills of this particular trainer, as well as his warmth, were the ingredients that finally allowed this group to proceed in a positive way. At the conclusion of the program, all twelve members felt that their group had been a very good experience.

Case 5

The idea to run a laboratory for widows and widowers came to Harvey a few years back, when he observed his father struggling for ways to restructure his life following his wife's painful death from cancer. Harvey had wished then for the existence of a group, like the one he was about to start, in an idyllic lodge high in the Colorado Rocky Mountains. The enrollment was encouraging: Actually, one-third to one-half of the group would be men. It should be an excellent program, Harvey thought, the breathtaking scenery was sure to uplift their sad hearts, and perhaps he could awaken in a few of the members the joy of childhood hobbies like fishing, painting, and drawing, leaf collecting, hiking, and maybe even camping.

What started out as such a wonderful idea almost turned into disaster because Harvey had forgotten a very important step in preparing for the event. He was already in the opening session when he realized that he might have made a mistake. Looking over the group of 18 men and women, he noticed a man, probably in his early sixties, who was breathing very heavily and using an inhaler off and on. Now, for the first time. the question arose in Harvey's mind, "Where is the nearest medical facility?" At the break he immediately contacted the staff of the lodge and learned that the nearest hospital was approximately two hours away and that there were no doctors' offices nearby. Harvey shrugged his shoulders, wrote the hospital telephone number down, and returned to the group. At the end of that evening's session, he made the appropriate announcement that if, for whatever reason, anyone was going to miss a group session that he must be informed beforehand. Should there be no prior notice of an individual's absence, he or someone else would seek out the absent group member. With these words he wished the group a good night and retired to his room to get some rest. Before sleeping, Harvey pulled out the group application forms, now that he could attach faces to names. He was pleased to note that people in the group seemed to have come from all walks of life. There was a postal clerk, a sales representative, an engineer, and a woman physician in partial retirement. The man with breathing difficulties was from Philadelphia, he was 65 years old and his name was Rudy. Harvey turned off the light and went to sleep but was soon awakened by urgent knocking at his door.

Rudy's roommate had come to tell Harvey that Rudy was having marked breathing troubles and was complaining of chest pain and left arm pain. The two rushed into Rudy's room and found him propped up in bed. His face had turned a grayish purple color and with terror in his eyes, he was gasping for air. Harvey instructed Rudy's roommate to get Ida, the physician who fortunately had not yet gone to bed. When Ida could not find Rudy's pulse, she quickly instructed the two men to move Rudy to the floor. While she gave him artificial respiration, she had Harvey apply pressure to Rudy's chest. Rudy's color improved rapidly with the CPR maneuvers. The hospital was notified of the emergency and a Life-Line helicopter soon fetched Rudy and flew him to the hospital. The experience was harrowing for Harvey. He realized then that the choice of a group session site must always include not only a peaceful and comfortable physical environment but also readily available medical help. Additionally, he learned from Ida that Rudy probably got into trouble because of the high altitude. This Philadelphian had been more or less medically stable at sea level, but in the Rockies, where his oxygen supply was decreased, his pulmonary condition had put an added strain on his heart. This led to the heart attack that could have killed him.

Case 6

Unfortunately, Harvey's problems were not over. On the fifth day of his program for the bereaved, a "dear, sweet woman" in her late forties who had lost her husband approximately a year earlier, began acting "strange." Thelma had been an active participant in the group. Her insight and comments had been useful to a number of the participants, and whenever someone expressed his or her pain, Thelma was one of the first to be there with either physical contact or words of comfort. Today she did not seem herself.

During the morning session, while Harvey was talking about various techniques to reduce stress, Thelma suddenly announced that she was tired of listening to stress reduction lectures. She had heard enough of those at the hospital where her husband had died, and those had been better lectures anyway. When the group members defended Harvey, she became belligerent, used obscene language, and then began to ramble something about young upstarts who think they know everything. "Nobody will listen to authority anymore. Irreverence is the main problem with our society." "Thank God my children aren't that way," she had "brought them up right" and so on.

Other group members urged Harvey to go on with his lecture. Harvey tried. However, eventually he was unable to ignore Thelma because she kept accompanying his talk with sarcastic remarks like, "Hear, hear" or "Is that what you think, honey boy?" Uncertain about what to do, Harvey stopped his talk (a structural, individual, low-intensity intervention). With the help of Ida and another group member, he got Thelma to her room. By this time Thelma had become combative and needed to be restrained. When Ida, the physician, went to the bathroom to get a cold, wet washcloth for Thelma's forehead she saw a bottle of insulin and a syringe on the counter of the bathroom cabinet. Putting two and two together, Ida surmised that Thelma was a long time insulin-dependent diabetic whose blood sugar had dropped suddenly into the hypoglycemic range. Without delay she ordered large amounts of orange juice and sugar for Thelma, and when it was brought, Ida insisted she drink the concoction. In the meantime Harvey was on the phone with the psychiatrist-consultant whose office was three hours away from the lodge by car. Because of the great distance, the psychiatrist recommended psychiatric hospitalization in the nearest hospital. Again a Life-Line helicopter was summoned. On its arrival the medics tested Thelma's blood sugar which was still too low. Rather than being taken to the psychiatric ward, Thelma was flown to the regional hospital for medical care.

Later Ida explained to the group that diabetics, when they have been on insulin for a long period of time, can develop sudden personality changes and psychotic behaviors with or without aggression when their blood sugar drops too low after their morning insulin. In people with more recent onset of diabetes, hypoglycemic episodes are relatively easy for the patient himself or herself to recognize. These individuals will complain of feeling shaky inside, of a racing heartbeat, cold sweats, and hunger for a considerable period before the brain dysfunction occurs. They may also visibly shake. Had Thelma not been given sugar quickly after the onset of her symptoms, her condition could have progressed to seizures and coma.

In talking with Ida about how problems like Thelma's could have been avoided, Ida encouraged Harvey to include medical questions on his laboratory application such as: Are you currently under the care of a physician for a medical or a psychiatric condition? Are you currently receiving any type of medication on a daily or near daily basis? Addresses and phone numbers of the treating physicians should also be requested, as well as the exact name of any medications taken, including the dosage, so that correct treatment can be given quickly should an emergency arise.

It is understandable that this particular group of bereaved men and women became especially alarmed over these two incidents. It brought back into the foreground the loss of their spouses and in some the hopelessness that their lives could ever again be satisfying. Therefore, Harvey needed to spend much more time in the laboratory on the grieving process than he had anticipated. He had hoped that he could move beyond the grief work and help the group members begin to structure their present-day lives and future in such a way that they would be looking for novel ways to regain some of life's past pleasures.

To get closer to his goal for the laboratory, he had each group member write down what they missed most in their lives since the death of their spouse (a structural, individual, low-intensity intervention). Small groups worked on lists of suggestions for how each person might fill these needs in the absence of their spouse. Each group member then chose a partner with whom they wanted to stay in contact after the laboratory came to a close. This was done in order to help the group members stick to their goals and report on their progress. The trainer, Harvey, also gave out his phone numbers so that if a pair had difficulty with their assignment they could contact him for help. A few of the pairs actually did call Harvey for help. Harvey took time to contact the others himself, thereby assuring himself that overall the program had been a success, although the process had been less than smooth and rather more protracted than Harvey had envisioned.

Case 7

Trust walks have been carried out in personal growth groups since the 1960s. On a trust walk, one person leads another who is blindfolded, an experience that can bring about significant learning both for the guide and the guided. Donald had paired up with Cindy. They had not chosen one another, they were the last two left after the other group members had paired up quickly for the exercise. Cindy, shy, in her early thirties, had chosen this program in order to help her learn to speak her mind more readily. She felt she had ideas that could help her advance in her company, if she could only learn to offer them at team meetings. Donald had so far been somewhat of a nonentity in the group. He had stated on his application form that he wanted to learn to communicate better with his employees, so that their productivity would be increased. For the most part, Donald had been sitting on the periphery of the group. There were times when he was observed to actually nod off. The trainer had been aware of Donald's withdrawn behavior but had not spoken to him directly in hopes that another group member would bring it up. It was the second afternoon of the six-and-one-half-day event. The group was struggling with inclusion issues and early control issues. The trust walk began (a structured experience).

Cindy had wanted to be the guide first on the trust walk, but Donald grabbed the scarf from her hands and tied it over her eyes saying, "I'll guide you first." As usual, Cindy did what was expected of her, even though (in retrospect) she realized that she detected alcohol on Donald's breath. The trainer had instructed them to take about twenty minutes for each trust walk. During this time, they were to pay attention to how it felt having to trust another person completely, or in the case of the guide, to have total responsibility for another human being. He also suggested that it might be interesting to expose the guided person to various perceptions, to see if being deprived of sight in any way affected the other senses.

Donald took Cindy firmly by the arm and guided her up some steps into another room, which she later learned was Donald's room. He had her feel smooth surfaces and rough surfaces, warm water and cold water, and try to tell pennies apart from nickels. Cindy was beginning to enjoy herself when Donald decided to give her a variety of fragrance experiences. He had her smell news print, his leather attaché, his shaving lotion, and then some alcohol which he had poured into a glass. Afterward, Cindy heard him drink something. Then Donald brought her safely down the steps and led her outside. Cindy was not sure in which direction Donald was leading her, but after a little while, Donald guided her into a car.

"There's somewhere I want to take you," he said, "but it's too far to walk." With Cindy blindfolded at his side, Donald drove off. Cindy's next awareness was that she was lying on the sidewalk looking up at a group of strangers. Her head was in severe pain. While putting pressure on her forehead, someone told her not to worry, that an ambulance had been called. Donald had run the red light and they had been in a collision. Other than a few scratches and bruises, Donald had escaped any significant injuries.

This "light and benign" exercise, a trust walk, had turned into a major incident for Cindy, Donald, the trainer, and the group as a whole. A concussion and a whiplash injury were minor in comparison to the emotional setback Cindy experienced. She blamed herself for the incident because once again she had not been assertive enough. More than ever, she saw herself as inadequate, destined to be so the rest of her life. In order to receive appropriate medical care, she was unable to finish the laboratory. In addition she had to take sick leave from work, and eventually needed to consult a psychiatrist to help her deal with a pervasive, lingering depression. When she got better, she sued Donald for damages.

The alcohol content in Donald's blood exceeded the legal limit, and because this was his second driving-while-under-the-influence conviction, he lost his driver's license and was incarcerated. From there he entered a twenty-eight-day alcohol rehabilitation program. The trainer had a difficult time finishing this laboratory. He had trouble sleeping, he worried about Cindy's health, and he blamed himself for not having picked up Donald's drinking earlier. He knew that should he ever organize a trust walk again, he would do it later in a group's development after he knew each group member better. At such a time perhaps he would be a better judge of how the pairing might work. Additionally, he determined that in the future he would be specific in the instruction that no one could go beyond the fence of the retreat center, and that he would be sure to remain on the premises while the exercise was underway. It so happened that he had taken the opportunity while the group was occupied with the trust walk to drive to a nearby drug store to pick up some toilet articles he had forgotten, and to sip an ice cream soda. He therefore was not available when the accident occurred, and the confusion was enhanced because he could not give information to the police who wondered why Cindy was driven blindfolded in a car.

Fortunately, this trainer had a good support system back home. Only with the help of his friends and colleagues with whom he stayed in contact on a twice-a-day basis, was he able to finish the laboratory and help the group deal with issues of trust. All the other group members had good experiences on their trust walks and if it had not been a significant emotional experience for them, it certainly had been fun. Cindy's experience with Donald however, reinforced the old truism that you "can't trust all people all of the time."

Even after the laboratory ended, the trainer remained in contact with Cindy on a regular basis to monitor her progress. It was he who suggested that she see a psychiatrist when he realized that she was getting more and more depressed. It is probably his rapport with Cindy (which developed mostly after she left the group) that spared his inclusion in the suit for damages.

Case 8

Dean was an unassuming, somewhat heavyset man in his mid-thirties who had come to a one-week group skills workshop with a T-group component. Back home he worked in the Human Resources department of a large firm. Dean had used his vacation time to attend this workshop and had paid for it out of his own pocket. His firm had placed him on probation because of poor productivity and chronic tardiness. In that Dean's work history had been poor for several years, and because he had been dismissed from several jobs, he decided to take part in this workshop in the hopes of improving the quality of his work. Although Dean did not contribute much in the group, he was the only participant who took notes of everything that went on. In the mornings he was consistently late while profusely offering excuses, claiming that he overslept.

Group members took turns leading a T-group. On the fifth day of the group, it was to be Dean's turn. On the fourth day, when Dean had not shown up one hour into the session, the trainer asked for a volunteer to check on Dean. Michael volunteered and went to look for Dean. A while later, Michael returned. He brought back an unshaven Dean and a package in a brown paper bag. Since the group was involved in scrutinizing a conflict that had occurred earlier between two members, the pair's arrival was noticed but not dealt with immediately.

Dean appeared listless and seemed to have trouble keeping his eyes open. The trainer had to take action, to find out what was wrong with Dean. She chose a check-in round, asking each person to say a sentence or two about how they were feeling at that particular point (a structural, individual, low-intensity intervention). When it was Dean's turn to give his check-in, he said he did not know how he was feeling. After a few seconds of silence he added, "I guess, 'not good' would sum it up." With those words he leaned back in his chair. Michael's turn was next. He described himself as feeling upset because of what he had found in Dean's room and he pointed to the brown paper bag.

When the check-in-round was completed, the trainer turned her attention to Michael and asked, "What's in the brown bag?" Michael opened the bag and pulled out a handgun. Everyone stared at the gun except for Dean whose eyes were downcast. The trainer asked Dean whether this was his gun and when Dean nodded, she asked him where he got it. Dean then told this story haltingly.

He had been carrying this gun with him for the past 1½ years. It was the gun that his father had used to kill himself when Dean was just 13 years old. His father had been involved in a series of wild business schemes and when they failed he took his life. For years Dean was very angry at his father for the suicide because of how it had affected his mother, his sister, and himself. However, lately he thought his father's decision to kill himself had not been such a bad one because, "life really is hardly worth living." Dean explained that his wife had left him because he could not hold a job. He still missed her very much. "Maybe if I can prove to her that I can be a reliable provider she'll come back."

Dean took a long time to say all of this. Between sentences he stopped and wiped his eyes. Sobbing, he said, "I'll know by tomorrow if I can get her back. If you approve of my design (for the workshop he was to do at his company when he returned), then I know it will get me off probation. Then she'll come back . . . but if you don't approve I'll know that I just don't have it in me to be a good group leader. Then . . . I'll just use this." He pointed to the gun.

Someone said, "Dean, you can't really mean that. How can you allow a workshop design to decide whether you are going to live or not?" Another participant ventured, "That's crazy, come on Dean, you just can't give up like that." The trainer interrupted and asked Dean whether he was receiving any therapy. Dean replied that he had been in therapy for the last 18 months but did not feel any better. "I guess I am just a failure all around." When the trainer inquired about whether he was on medication, Dean said his therapist did not believe in the "magic of pills" and felt that Dean had not come to terms with his father's death and that this was why he was feeling so low. To this the trainer replied, "You know Dean, I think that you are just terribly depressed, and that's why you can't function at work, and why you have to sleep so much (a conceptual, individual, high-intensity intervention). There's help for depression now. I'll get in touch with the psychiatrist consultant we have in residence and talk this over with him, since I'm not a doctor. But I feel sure, Dean, that you can be helped. In the meantime, I'd like you to give me that handgun. I will keep it safe and I will take good care of it, but it really is against the rules of our program to have a gun around. So please give it to me for safe keeping." With that she stretched out her hand. Dean handed the gun over, then broke into deep sobbing. After the trainer made sure that there were people available to take care of Dean, she called the psychiatrist consultant and arranged an appointment for him.

Dean had indicated on his application form that he was in therapy. A letter had been sent to his therapist requesting the therapist's consent for Dean's participation in the lab. The therapist had recommended him without reservations.

The training laboratory's psychiatrist was able to see Dean that afternoon. He determined that Dean was suffering from manic depressive illness for which he should receive medication. He considered Dean an immediate suicidal risk and therefore recommended immediate hospitalization. Dean did not want to be hospitalized because he felt he would surely lose his job if it became known that he was in a psychiatric hospital. His wife was consulted and several alternatives were considered. The final decision was to admit Dean to a psychiatric ward in a medical hospital in his hometown, so that he could be treated for manic depressive illness in addition to dealing with his marital problems.

While Dean was waiting to be picked up by his sister, to be taken to the hospital, a group member stayed with Dean continuously. Dean promised that he would voluntarily go into the hospital on his arrival at home, and was told if he did not do so that he could be committed against his will. The gun was not given to either Dean or his sister. Another group member who happened to live in the same town took it, at the end of the program, to Dean's wife for safe keeping.

After Dean departed the group was somber. They realized how close they had been to witnessing and experiencing a major disaster. The trainer allowed time for group members to express their reactions. Two said they had lost distant family members through suicide and recounted what impact the sudden deaths had on them. Later on that evening the trainer called Dean's sister to confirm that Dean was indeed admitted to the hospital. The group sent Dean a card and fruit basket. A month later the trainer received a note from Dean. His depression had resolved, he was taking Lithium now, and his wife had moved back with him. He thanked the trainer profusely for her help. Soon he would be returning to work. He asked for permission to call her should he have any questions about the design for his next big group event.

Case 9

Marcia was described by her trainer as very bright, articulate, clever, and creative. Unfortunately she consistently used those skills in order to control and manipulate other participants. Marcia repeatedly "played therapist," interpreting participants' behavior to them whether they wanted to hear it or not, refused to share her own feelings, and cross-examined anyone who attempted to confront her. In terms of brightness and one-up-manship none of the participants could match her.

Her response to trainer intervention aimed at helping her learn to "play fair" and to express feelings rather than judgments was to withdraw and sulk. That did not last long though. She soon was back again, finding ways to have other group members interact with her and be interrogated by her.

Her extreme dominance reached its zenith when, in support groups, each group of five was allocated a specific, limited amount of time to serve as consultants for each of its members. Marcia's group, astonishingly, was unable to enforce time limitations and Marcia usurped the entire time period for her own issues. Afterward, when questioned by a trainer, her group members confided that when they attempted to move her off center stage, she resisted so strenuously that it soon became clear that she could not be dealt with in a reasonable or efficient way. Her behavior in the group was described as "extremely destructive." She used her talents and bright-ness in order to enhance her own power and was completely oblivious to the needs of others.

At that point, when it became clear to her seasoned trainers that in spite of their repeated high-intensity conceptual interventions Marcia would continue to be a problem to manage, they decided to consult with the psychiatrist. When the psychiatrist heard about the difficulties she felt that she needed to see Marcia herself in order to hopefully get another perspec-tive. The problem now was how to get Marcia to cooperate with that plan. Bill, the younger of her trainers, volunteered to ask Marcia. Before the next group session began he took Marcia aside and spoke to her very frankly, telling her that he really admired her intellect and felt that she could make an outstanding contribution to the learning of the group but that she was going about it in a way that turned people off. Marcia was vaguely able to agree that others seemed uncomfortable with her style. He than asked her if she would consent to see the psychiatrist consultant in that both he and his co-trainer had tried to help her to be more effective in the group but apparently had not been able to do so. To his relief Marcia agreed to do so.

In discussion with the psychiatrist consultant Marcia disclosed that she was planning a separation from her husband and that there was some threat of losing custody of her children. She also disclosed a suicide attempt three weeks before beginning the laboratory. In addition, her supervisor at work had put her on probation because she had single-handedly changed pro-duction flow procedures in her section without first consulting with her superiors. Through talking with the psychiatrist consultant she was able to see more clearly that her domineering style was causing difficulties in all of her relationships—that is, in her family, at work, and in this workshop. Her immediate response to that insight was a decision to leave the workshop. Marcia apparently felt rejected and ashamed. The psychiatrist persuaded her not to make a hasty decision, and told her that such a decision was best made with input from her trainers. Throughout the evaluation by the psychiatrist, Marcia had been cooperative and was able to listen. She had even cried when reporting her fear of losing her children. Her controlling, one-up style exhibited in the group was simply not there.

The psychiatrist returned to the trainers with that information. Because Marcia's home support system was apparently weak and because Marcia had demonstrated an ability to hear feedback, the staff team felt that it would be safer for Marcia to stay in the workshop. They decided to encourage her to stay in the workshop if she would agree to certain conditions. Marcia was to abstain from conceptual statements. She was encouraged instead to make experiential statements about herself or give positive feedback to others. Any conceptual statement she wanted to make she could write down and once a day a maximum of five minutes of group time was to be given to her to present it to the group if she chose to do so. The group could use the following ten minutes to verbalize their own analysis of the day's events. In addition Marcia was to touch base with the psychiatrist on a daily basis to deal with any feelings that might be stirred up by the restrictions on her and to see if the restrictions needed to be in place for another day. Anytime the group would break into smaller groups the trainer, Bill would monitor the small group in which she participated.

It turned out that Marcia was able to finish the program. In fact during the final thirty hours of the program, after she had shown enough control under the very structured system, she was able to return to unrestricted participation and did not abuse the privilege. Her conceptual input about the group process had always been insightful and she earned the respect of at least some of the group members because of it. During an informal talk, Bill suggested to her that she continue her personal growth quest by going into therapy at home. She bristled at the idea. It was not until the psychiatrist discussed with her the possible benefits from therapy that Marcia promised to do so.

It became very clear that one of Marcia's main problems was that she did not trust men. Both the trainers were men and the majority of the group members were men. When she had been put into a small group with four other men, her most severely dominating behavior emerged, which ultimately led to the consultation with the psychiatrist. It was indeed fortunate that the outside psychiatrist at that particular time happened to be female. Marcia was quickly able to develop a trusting relationship with her and could tolerate interpretive, conceptual interventions from her and use them.

The reader may question the wisdom of continuing Marcia in the program. She occupied a very large amount of staff's time. When the trainers in collaboration with the psychiatrist consultant had decided to give her the option of staying in the program, they were aware of the time commitment they were about to make. However, in that an on-site psychiatrist as well as two trainers were available for this workshop, they felt that they could handle the challenge and hopefully make a real difference to Marcia. A solo trainer with an off-site consultant probably could not have kept her in the laboratory.

Considering the severity of the structure imposed by the trainers upon Marcia's overtalking and intrusiveness, the group might have felt intimidated. That did not happen. Instead the group became more lively and freer, possibly because clear boundaries had been set. Apparently, giving the group members clear guidelines for acceptable group behavior was helpful in this instance.

Marcia's behavior looked initially like a Quadrant II, blind distress reaction. However, when she was able to open up with the woman psychiatrist, it turned out to be primarily a more malleable hidden anxiety and distress reaction as described in Quadrant III. This participant's life stress was severe at the time she chose to do the workshop. She frequently felt very insecure, overwhelmed, and depressed. She apparently tried to cope with her distress by intermittently swinging into domineering behaviors, especially with males, in order to prove to herself that she had competence and that she could control her life.

Case 10

Joy, a British resident of Hong Kong appeared anxious and tense in the workshop on Working Together: Dealing with Conflict between Men and Women. She had come to the United States in order to spend her summer taking various training groups in connection with her work and her interest in the field of family therapy. This was her third workshop in the span of six weeks. She was scheduled to attend one more training course prior to returning to Hong Kong.

Joy was an actively participating group member, but she tended to bring up personal anecdotes from conflicts with her father when she was a child while the rest of the group dealt with conflictual situations at work. In addition, she relentlessly implored the group leader to let her husband, an in-house human resources consultant for a large corporation in Hong Kong, join this group. Unlike Joy, he had just come to the United States to spend what was left of the summer with his wife. Being sensitive to Joy's special status as a foreigner and in the hope that she would feel more at ease in the workshop, the trainer permitted Hugh, Joy's husband, to join the group one and one-half days into the program. However her discomfort did not improve. She progressively became less verbal and at times would have tears in her eyes when others talked about conflictual relationships with which they had to deal. Hugh was quietly attentive to the group's work and contributed sparingly but was to the point, especially in the didactic sessions of the program. Early on the fourth day, the trainer noted that Joy's eyes appeared to be swollen and that she was pale. When another group member chose Joy's husband to role play someone who was trying to work out a conflict with a female colleague and Hugh did it very skillfully and sensitively, Joy broke down crying and shouted, "Why don't you do that with me? You never listen to what I have to say—you act like I don't exist, like what I feel does not matter." Apparently Joy had had a hidden agenda for choosing this workshop—she had hoped that it would fix their marriage.

The remainder of that group session was thoroughly derailed. Hugh tried to calm his wife down telling her that they could work on their problems later; she would not hear it and tried to give examples of how Hugh was insensitive to her. A number of group members tried to be helpful by asking questions. It took several interventions by the trainer to point out that marital therapy was not what this workshop was designed for and that instead the workshop was designed to make them better manage conflict between men and women in the workplace and so on (conceptual, group, high-intensity interventions). Finally Joy settled down. Hugh was obviously embarrassed by the events of the morning. With everyone present, the trainer asked Joy if she would be willing to see the psychiatrist consultant that afternoon with Hugh "to talk things over." Both agreed to that plan and for the remainder of the workshop, Joy and Hugh had daily sessions to help them with their marital problems. There was only one occasion later on in the workshop when Joy tried to bring up the troubled relationship with her husband again, however the trainer immediately stopped her. Except for that minor interruption the group's focus remained educational and on the workplace and the trainer was able to encapsulate the couple's distress outside of the group.

This case illustrates a number of factors that can create incidents: Although the workshop description clearly stated that it was a program to deal with gender conflict at the workplace, Joy misinterpreted the workshop goals. Also her emotional liability had probably been heightened because she had been through several workshops in rapid succession just prior to the current one. In retrospect, it is apparent that the trainer should not have bowed to Joy's insistence that her husband be included in the workshop. Had the trainer inquired why Joy was so tense he might have learned about her marital distress, although Joy may not have been totally clear about the cause of her anxiety herself. The trainer advised the couple not to attend another program following this workshop and instead to spend the rest of the summer in a relaxing environment. They planned to continue their marital therapy following their return to Hong Kong.

Conclusion

Ten case studies were presented in some detail to give the reader examples of what types of clinical incidents can and do occur in laboratory education. The choice of cases was intentionally skewed towards incidents of greater severity to give students and trainers alike an opportunity to think through intervention options in those difficult cases. Throughout the examples trainer interventions were analyzed using the Cohen and Smith Intervention Cube.

8. THE TRAINER

Much has been said here about the vulnerabilities a participant brings to a program that may predispose him or her to a clinical distress incident. But the participant's vulnerability is only one (albeit important) piece of the clinical incident equation. The group's composition also affects a participant's stress level. Unfortunately, there are limits to what can be done to change the cast of people who happen to come together for a particular program. However, a trainer's conduct in the group is surely of equal, or even greater importance than the other two factors. Let us concentrate, therefore, in this chapter on the facet of laboratory training that has the greatest potential to be controllable, which is the trainer.

Trainers need to be aware that their behavior has a greater influence on how a participant feels than the behavior of any other person in the group. It is the trainer's role as the actual and perceived authority figure that tilts the power balance so decidedly in his or her direction. Any word, any judgement, any gesture, any touch by the trainer is carefully observed by participants and weighed by most of them as to whether or not it spells approval, indifference, or rejection of them as individuals. There are usually only a few participants in any group who are relatively free of this kind of need for approval and who can maintain their self-esteem in the face of perceived or real disapproval or rejection by others. The rest possess various degrees of vulnerability to disapproval, either because their self-esteem is fragile or because their partial loss of identity amidst the ambiguity of the group is quite different from their day-to-day roles at work and at home, which give them emotional security.

Trainers can try to minimize their role of power and influence; however, they cannot fully escape it, nor should they. The power of the leader's role is necessary to manage the group. A laissez-faire leadership style can be a serious liability for the safety of participants, as well as for the success of the program itself.

Ethical Use of the Trainer Role

Whenever a person has power over others, that power can be abused and cause harm. Harm to participants is most likely to occur when a trainer has a psychological need to control participants or to be loved by them. The mature trainer never uses participants for his or her own psychological gain but works diligently towards the psychological gain of all participants in the program. This may mean that the trainer will permit participants to take center stage, to criticize him or her, and even to ascribe less than noble motives to the trainer. Also, the mature trainer can be nondefensive when a weakness or a mistake he or she may have made is uncovered during the course of the event. Sarcasm and humor at the expense of the participant, or name calling or labeling by the trainer have no place in laboratory education. They violate the trust that participants place in a trainer.

It is an abuse of the trainer's power to force a participant to do any psychological work he or she is not ready to do—that is, force group norms of self-disclosure on a reticent participant, impose the trainer's own value system (e.g., what to discuss or how much affect to display), or own cultural norms. This can be especially problematic when working with members of the opposite gender or with participants of a different race or ethnicity. Criticizing a participant's behavior or presumed attitude is an abuse of power, unless the trainer first communicates to the participant that he or she is appreciated and cared about. Lip service is not enough; there must be a genuinely trusting relationship between a trainer and participant before criticism can foster learning. It is also an abuse of power for a trainer to engage a participant in verbal or nonverbal exercises without giving that person the choice about engaging in such activity. The same is true for a trainer who insists that an exercise be completed even though the participant indicates a desire to stop and begins showing signs of distress. Careful use of the power of the trainer role is important whether the participant is working on a sales presentation, management style, or interpersonal skills. It is often difficult to decide how far to push a participant, or allow a participant to be pushed by the group, towards learning. When a trainer listens intently for what the participant wants, and is willing to subordinate his or her own desire or need to see the participant gain insight or change, a safe climate for learning is created.

In the past fifteen years, another type of abuse by some therapists and some trainers has been publicized; namely, the sexual seduction of patients or participants. This represents an extreme abuse of power, and often is based on transference or countertransference reactions. These liaisons are usually short-lived and are not healthy relationships—even if they are desired by both parties.

Needless to say, it is the patient or participant who pays the price emotionally. Major distress reactions can occur as a consequence. The imbalance in power in laboratory learning groups and the implicit contract between trainer and participants (i.e., the trainer is responsible for the emotional well-being of the participants) removes sexual relationships between trainer and participant from the category of "anything is permissible between two consenting adults short of physical injury."

The need to be loved is not limited to the sexual arena. Trainers may enjoy the power role as trainers because the group gives them a stage to exhibit their talents—how witty they can be, how clever, how brilliant. Whenever a trainer succeeds in being adored by his participants, the participants have likely been abused. They come to the program to develop themselves, not to be used to boost the trainer's ego. Trainers who take excessive floor time or excessively engage in funny antics for amusement may be attention-seeking in a way that is at best not helpful to participants, and actually may be harmful to them.

Trainer Transference and Countertransference

Transference reactions were mentioned earlier in this chapter and discussed at length in Chapter 2. Transference reactions are often triggered by very minor similarities between a person from the past and the person in the present—tone of voice, body build or posture, or a specific attitude displayed. Psychologically, the person on whom the transference is projected may have a very different makeup from the person of the past. Certainly the role relationship will be totally different. Yet all the emotional baggage of that early relationship gets transferred onto the new person without examination to see if it really fits.

If the transference reaction is a positive one it generally does not do a great deal of harm. A very strong positive transference reaction to a specific participant can, however, result in favoritism in the group and arouse the jealousy and rivalry of other participants. Negative transference reactions are a major problem if they are not quickly identified and, at least privately, acknowledged.

A trainer may have had an alcoholic father. When he learns that a participant was carried to his room early in the morning by other group members because he had gotten drunk, the trainer may react with excessive anger, disdain, and rejection of that participant, as if that participant were his alcoholic father. He may, therefore, not be able to provide the needed support or might even undermine the support the group is willing to give this overwrought person.

Another example is a trainer, whose mentally ill mother dressed seductively and was occasionally promiscuous, who may ascribe that same behavior to a female participant who comes to dinner on the final evening of a program in a somewhat revealing outfit. Or a more subtle transference may be that a trainer finds herself suddenly angry with a participant who will not deal with his feelings because she is still angry with her father who could not or would not deal with his feelings. The problem with a transference reaction is that it is out of step with reality; the actual attitudes and emotional makeup of the participant in the here-and-now may require a very different approach than was the case with the person in the past. The participant may be burdened with false attributes. Therefore his or her needs are not met. It is not hard to see how clinical incidents might develop if the process is not quickly recognized for what it is. The hallmark of a transference reaction is that it leads to very strong feelings even though the behavior exhibited by the person in the present is not that far out of the norm. Also, immediate strong emotional responses to a participant's demeanor without real knowledge of the person (e.g., a brief encounter in the opening session) could well be based on transference.

It behooves the trainer to examine his or her strong negative feelings in order to determine the source. Having a co-trainer in the group certainly makes that process easier. If staff team building has been successful, a trainer will be able to and should use his or her co-trainer to check out a suspected transference reaction to a participant. Whenever possible, the co-trainer should then deal primarily with that particular participant, to assure that the participant's real concerns are addressed.

Should a trainer in a solo training role recognize that he or she has a negative transference reaction to a participant, he or she needs to be very careful. Intuition is not useful at times like this. Due to the transference reaction, intuition will not serve reliably. Without this important guide, the trainer should probably avoid a confrontation with that particular participant and be careful not to coerce the group to do the confrontation for him- or herself. Instead, the trainer might make it a point to be warm with that special participant. After all, this participant has helped the trainer to learn more about him- or herself and find out where the inner unfinished business is. Therapy may be needed to help a trainer come to terms with some childhood emotional burdens.

It is probably not possible to experience new people in our lives without some transference of feelings that belong to our past. As long as they do not distort our ability to respond appropriately to present realities, they are useful and give us that quick first impression. As we learn more about a person these first impressions then must be modified to fit reality. When stuck in transference reaction, a trainer will be unable to make those necessary adjustments.

Countertransference reactions occur when a trainer develops strong emotional responses to a participant's transference reaction to her or him. An example would be that a trainer is disliked strongly by one of the participants because the trainer reminded the participant of his or her rigid, authoritarian father when he or she refused to alter the program schedule as some group members requested. The participant shouts, "You're running this event like a Nazi camp!" The trainer, a Jew, is enraged and proceeds to shout at the participant in staccato sentences what Nazis are really like, reaching back into his childhood memories of the concentration camps, while the group watches the outbursts in alarm. The participant, through transference, triggered the trainer's rage about what he had to endure as a helpless child years before and the trainer transferred his rage against his Nazi commander onto the participant.

Trainer Projection

Projection is another mental process that can result in clinical distress incidents if the trainer is not aware of what is occurring. As mentioned in Chapter 2, racial prejudice and scapegoating are often based on projection. Projection is also the mechanism that underlies a former alcoholic's disdain, for example, for unreformed alcoholics. Generally, the stronger a person is fighting a negative attribute within the self, the stronger the dislike will be of a person who displays that attribute or who is presumed to have that attribute. An example is the female trainer who finds herself strongly disliking a young woman who dresses in a glamourous fashion and talks excessively, seemingly to attract attention. As a child, this trainer had been taught that to look in a mirror was vain and that vanity is bad. Now as an adult, she still dresses unobtrusively so as not to draw attention to herself. She is only dimly aware that part of her would find it fun to be glamourous, to be noticed. The male co-trainer, on the other hand, did not find the participant's behavior that deviant. The female trainer, on the other hand, had been almost ready to address the "attention-seeking" behavior as dysfunctional and comment about it in the group. It was not until the co-trainer expressed a different perspective that the trainer became aware of the source of her dislike of the participant. She was then able to start seeing the participant in a different light.

Co-Training

From the above, it is apparent that solo training can be more risky for the participant because a possible check-and-balance system is missing. Solo training should never be attempted until a trainer has learned the theories of group processes, understands psychological processes, and has gained a great deal of experience in laboratory education. This experience includes investing time as a participant in a variety of laboratory programs, working under supervision as a trainer, and working as a co-trainer. Examining the apprentice trainer's actions and reactions in the group for projective and transference reactions needs to be a definite part of any trainer's education. Co-training will not automatically decrease the risk of harm to participants. The trainers must have built enough trust with each other that they can confront each other on how participants are handled. They must be able to be nondefensive with one another so that they can ask for advice, help, and clarification. They must be in a learning stance— wanting to know about any projections or transference reactions they might have as a way of understanding themselves better and becoming more competent professionals.

This kind of team building takes time. How much time is needed will depend on the circumstances and individuals involved. When two trainers co-train repeatedly, less time will be needed. Working with the same trainer repeatedly, however, may also be a liability if the pair begins to assume they know what to expect of each other and are not truly in a learning mode.

The only situation that can be more risky for a participant in laboratory education than a solo trainer who is blind to his or her projections and transferences, is a colluding co-trainer team in which neither trainer looks for transferences and projections in the other, and who dare not confront one another even when they do notice a potential problem.

Working as a total staff team or with a co-trainer has another hazard that was previously mentioned. That is unresolved conflicts between staff members. This problem is more likely to occur when trainer teams are chosen by a person outside the team or assigned organizationally, than when the trainers mutually seek each other for the laboratory event. The mutual selection is more likely to team people who not only have positive relationships but who also share common views about training. This can also increase the conceptual integration of the program. Conflicted or split training teams generally make for less than cohesive programs, because trainers, consciously or unconsciously, will prevent cohesiveness in the group. Unresolved issues about racism and sexism are also likely to spill into the laboratory community. Participants are deprived of an opportunity to learn about these pervasive human problems when, because of team conflict, the staff steers the group away from dealing with the problem or deals with it very poorly. This may result in clinical incidents or escalate distress among participants that the staff will be ill-equipped to handle until staff members have finally dealt with whatever problem exists among its own members.

Trainer Preparedness

Training is stressful—it requires an alertness and openness to each participant's emotional state at that particular point in his or her life. A trainer who has trained a number of programs in succession is just as likely to create incidents as the participant who enrolls in several programs in succession. It is grandiose to assume that a trainer can have so much in the way of emotional reserves that he or she can train several emotionally intense programs in succession without cost. In such circumstances, the trainer frequently is unable to be patient with participants' tentative behaviors. A hardening of the trainer's expressed affect and a generally decreased ability to listen attentively to the participants' needs occurs, which can make training more risky for the participant. Also, fatigue is likely to cause a trainer to be less introspective, and therefore less open to self-examination for inappropriate emotional responses to participants.

As stated in Chapter 4, people who become experienced in the field of laboratory training (and therapy) often develop a sort of immunity. It is all too easy to lose touch with the emotional enormity of the unfreezing-changing-refreezing process. Over time, trainers easily get desensitized to the emotions of others whether the setting is an organizational sales training program or publicly offered interpersonal skills group. When this occurs, the trainer is less likely to detect difficulties and work appropriately with participants who are distressed. It is also likely that, over time, experienced trainers will stop seeking or accepting feedback about their behavior in the group. Participants are reluctant to tell difficult trainers about dysfunctional behavior such as not listening, overtalking, or lack of empathy.

It is only through regular participation in laboratory programs, as members rather than staff, that trainers can stay in touch with the power of the dynamics at work. This also ensures that trainers will receive feedback about themselves, in that participants are much less reluctant to provide it to their fellow members. Because this reality-testing and self-awareness opportunity is so crucial to good performance as a trainer, we call it *self-renewal*.

Training of Trainers

As discussed in Chapter 1, laboratory education evolved from the work of some psychologists and a philosopher. Psychiatrists and educators had early roles, too. The interdisciplinary nature of affective education is one of the problems in finding comprehensive and in-depth training programs for becoming a laboratory trainer.

The subject matter in Chapter 2 (Theoretical Foundations) lays out the kinds of knowledge—and the skills inferred from that subject matter knowledge—needed by trainers. Certainly, a competent group leader would be thoroughly grounded in theories of group dynamics and group development. In this book, Schutz's group development theory was reviewed, but no mention was made of dynamic theory, such as the work of Bion (1961). We tend to favor dynamic theories that assume unconscious processes because analytic concepts are so rooted in that assumption.

A knowledge of the biology as well as the psychology of stress is important in that the group leader must deal with the whole person in the program. Indeed, the clues to detecting stress and distress are often seen in the biological and physiological manifestations of the participant.

The concepts from analytic psychology are not so difficult to understand as they are to apply. That is why *supervision* (the term used for observation or consultation in clinical training) is so important in acquiring the needed competencies. Although one can attend workshops in some of the knowledge areas (e.g., stress management), clinical supervision is only available in professional internships or residencies. Perhaps the best way to acquire the level of competence needed for laboratory training is to apprentice oneself to well-trained clinicians. Certainly the reader is again advised to read the books by Strean (1985) and Laughlin (1979) suggested in Chapter 2.

This is not to say that clinical psychologists or psychiatrists are competent laboratory educators by virtue of their traditional training. Many programs have little emphasis on groups, and group therapy is not group training. Over time, the importance of groups has become better appreciated and more attention is given in some schools to this subject.

The group leader must have a concept of change in mind when working in laboratory training. We have used Lewin's theory in this book because it is so classical. There is a resurgence of interest in his field theory today and several Lewin societies have been formed as of this writing.

The above discussion illustrates why collaboration is probably the key to learning to be a competent laboratory group leader. The prospective trainer is encouraged to pursue learning in whatever ways are possible because no single way will suffice. The rigor of formal academic courses in such areas as personality theory, counselling, and group dynamics is quite beneficial. Learning by association with competent trainers is extremely beneficial. Workshops and formal nonacademic programs that are of high quality are certainly part of the process of becoming a competent trainer. Self-study can be designed with the help of colleagues who are well trained in the area of inquiry.

Peer Review

The unique opportunity for trainers to grow and develop personally and professionally through peer review during and after programs is, in the experience of the authors, seldom captured. Busy lives, airline schedule restrictions, fatigue, and eagerness to get home lead to a tacit agreement among staff members to say only positive things to each other or to have only a limited staff review of the program or themselves. There may be a suggestion that the staff review itself at a later date, but the most useful data for review, the experiential component, diminishes rapidly after the event is over. Also, because of cost and logistics, a review reunion is unlikely to occur. It is advisable, if at all possible, to schedule a staff review day following the close of the program. Staff can relax, forget about dashing to the plane, engage in recreation and "come down" from the program the afternoon or the evening of the program's close. The following day, appropriate time and effort can be invested in a real learning opportunity.

Conclusion

In this final chapter we have focused on the trainer as an individual and as a key variable in preventing and managing distress reactions of participants. The power of the trainer in a group makes it incumbent upon that person to operate ethically and be self-aware. Lack of self-awareness, like ignorance of the law, is no excuse. The dynamics of transference, counter-transference and projection as they might affect trainers, and the value of having a co-trainer in preventing the dysfunction of those dynamics were discussed. Working on staff of successive intense programs diminishes the trainer's capacity to perform and can increase the risk factor. The need for doing peer review in a sensitive way and the training of trainers were the final sections of this chapter.

In conclusion, the purpose of this book has been to provide some assistance in preventing, recognizing and managing people and dynamics that are counterproductive to learning. The vast majority of people who engage in laboratory education programs, as discussed in the Preface, have no difficulty managing their stress. As discussed in Chapter 1, the laboratory method is in widespread use. The popularity of the method is the result of the enormous gains it has achieved in facilitating learning. It is clearly the method of choice because of the results it has produced. The fact that corporations, governments, churches, and other major organizations have adopted the method in such a widespread way is evidence that it is simply good business to use such an effective method.

For individuals who have participated in this learning method, very few do not have instant recall of the powerful "aha" of self-discovery, which is the kind of learning that truly changes lives. Good practice in combination with such a beneficial learning method inevitably succeeds.

REFERENCES

Bales, R. F., & Shils, E. A. (Eds.). (1953). *Working papers in the theory of action.* Glencoe: Free Press.

Beck, A. T., Rush, A. J., Shaw, B. F., & Emery, G. (1979). *Cognitive therapy of depression.* New York: Guilford Press.

Benne, K. D., Bradford, L. P., Gibb, J. R., & Lippitt, R. O. (1975). *The laboratory method of changing and learning.* Palo Alto, CA: Science and Behavior Books.

Bion, W. R. (1961). *Experiences in groups.* New York: Basic Books.

Braaten, L. J. (1979). Some ethical dilemmas in sensitivity training, encounter groups and related activities. *Scandinavian Journal of Psychology, 20,* 81-91.

Brazelton, T. B., & Freedman, D. G. (1974). Manual to accompany Cambridge newborn behavioral and neurological scales. In G. B. A. Stoelinga & J. J. Van Der Werff (Eds.), *Normal and abnormal development of brain and behavior.* Leiden: Leiden University Press.

Brown, G. T., & Harris, T. (1978). *Social origins of depression: A study of psychotic disorder in women.* New York: Free Press.

Burns, D. D. (1980). *Feeling good—The new mood therapy.* New York: William Morrow.

Cohen, A. M., & Smith, R. D. (1976). *The critical incident in growth groups.* California: University Associates.

Cohen, F. (1981). Stress and bodily illness. *Psychiatric Clinics of North America, 4*(2), 269-286.

Ellis, A., & Harper, R. A. (1975). *The new guide to rational living.* Hollywood: Wilshire Publishing.

Freud, A. (1937). *The ego and the mechanisms of defense.* London: Hogarth.

Glass, L. L., Kirsch, M. A., & Parris, F. N. (1977). Psychiatric disturbances associated with Erhard seminars training: I. A report of cases. *American Journal of Psychiatry, 134,* 245-247.

Gottschalk, L. A., & Pattison, E. M. (1969). Psychiatric perspective on T-groups and the laboratory movement: An overview. *American Journal of Psychiatry, 126*, 91-107.

Higgitt, A. C., & Murray, R. M. (1983). A psychotic episode following Erhard seminars training. *Acta Psychiatrica Scandinavia, 67*, 436-439.

Kernberg, O. F. (1978a). Regression in organizational leadership. *Psychiatry, 42*, 21-38.

Kernberg, O. F. (1978b). Leadership and organizational functioning: Organizational regression. *International Journal of Group Psychotherapy, 28*, 3-25.

Kirsch, M. A., & Glass, L. L. (1977). Psychiatric disturbances associated with Erhard seminars training: II. Additional cases and theoretical considerations. *American Journal of Psychiatry, 134*, 1254-1258.

Klein, M. (1975). *Envy, gratitude and other works.* New York: Dell.

Laughlin, H. P. (1979). *The ego and its defenses.* New York: Jason Aronson.

Lewin, K. (1951). *Field theory in social science.* New York: Harper.

Lewin, K. (1958). Group decision and social change. In MacCoby, E. E., Newcomb, T. M., & Hartley, E. L. (Eds.), *Readings in social psychology.* New York: Holt, Rinehart & Winston.

Lieberman, M. A., Yalom, I. D., & Miles, M. B. (1973). *Encounter groups: First facts.* New York: Basic Books.

Luft, J. (1963). *Group process: An introduction to group dynamics.* Palo Alto, CA: National Press.

Malcolm, A. I. (1973). On the psychiatric and social implications of sensitivity training. *Canadian Psychiatric Association Journal, 18*, 527-531.

Marrow, A. J. (1969). *The practical theorist.* New York: Basic Books.

Moos, R. H., & Van Dort, B. (1979). Student physical symptoms and the social climate of college living groups. *American Journal of Community Psychology, 7*, 31-43.

Resnick, H., & Jaffee, B. (1982). The physical environment and social welfare. *Social Casework: The Journal of Contemporary Social Work*, 354-362.

Ross, W. D., Kligfeld, M., & Whitman, R. W. (1971). Psychiatrists, patients, and sensitivity groups. *Archives of General Psychiatry, 25*, 178-180.

Rutter, M. (1981). Stress, coping and development: Some issues and some questions. *Journal of Child Psychology and Psychiatry, 22*(4), 323-356.

Sale, I., Budtz-Olsen, I., Craig, G., & Kalua, R. (1980). Acute psychosis precipitated by encounter group experiences. *Medical Journal of Australia, 1*, 157-158.

Schutz, W. C. (1958). *Firo: A three-dimensional theory of interpersonal behavior.* New York: Rinehart.

Seashore, C. (1968). What is sensitivity training? *NTL Institute News and Reports, 2*, 1-2.

Selye, H. (1974). *Stress without distress.* New York: J. B. Lippincott.

Shadish, W. R. (1980). Non-verbal interventions in clinical groups. *Journal of Consulting and Clinical Psychology, 48*, 164-168.

Singer, D. L., Astrachan, B. M., Gould, L. J., & Klein, E. B. (1975). Boundary management in psychological work with groups. *Journal of Applied Behavioral Science, 11*, 137-176.

Spitz, R. (1946). *The psychoanalytic study of the child* (Vol. 2). New York: International Universities Press.

Stafford, L. L. (1977). Scapegoating. *American Journal of Nursing, 77*, 406-409.

Stone, W. N., & Tieger, M. E. (1971). Screening for T-groups: The myth of healthy candidates. *American Journal of Psychiatry, 127*, 61-66.

Strean, H. S. (1985). *Resolving resistances in psychotherapy.* New York: John Wiley.

Torgersen, S. (1980). Personality and experience in an encounter-group. *Scandinavian Journal of Psychology, 21,* 139-141.

Vaillant, G. E. (1977). *Adaptation to life.* Boston: Little, Brown.

Vestre, N. D., Greene, R. L., & Marks, M. W. (1978). Psychological adjustment of persons seeking sensitivity group experiences. *Psychological Reports, 42,* 1295-1298.

Walsh, B. W. (1975). Some theories of person/environment interaction. *Journal of College Student Personnel, 16,* 107-113.

Wechsler, I. R., Messarik, F., & Tannenbaum, R. (1962). The self in process: A sensitivity training emphasis. In I. R., Wechsler & E. H. Shein (Eds.). *Issues in training.* Washington, DC: National Education Association and National Training Laboratories.

Wilkinson, C. B., & O'Connor, W. A. (1982). Human ecology and mental illness. *American Journal of Psychiatry, 139,* 985-990.

Yalom, I. D., & Lieberman, M. A. (1971). A study of encounter group casualties. *Archives of General Psychiatry, 25,* 16-30.

INDEX

ABOUT THE AUTHORS

Birge D. Reichard (Ph.D., University of Maryland) is a Psychologist and an Associate Professor of Organization Behavior at The American University of Washington, D.C. He is also President of Berkeley Developmental Resources, Inc., which is a structured network of consultants in organization behavior and human resource development working in the United States, Canada, and the United Kingdom. He was a senior manager in human resources with Xerox Canada and held both operating and internal consulting positions with the Bell System. He is a former Vice President and Professional Director of the NTL Institute for Applied Behavioral Science. Through his management and consulting experience in more than fifty organizations in the United States, Canada, United Kingdom, and Mexico, he has gained an exceptional understanding of issues facing work groups and organizations in today's complex environment. Dr. Reichard has worked extensively with groups, especially work groups, and executive teams which are the basis of his commitment to this book.

Christiane M. F. Siewers (M.D., Bowman-Gray School of Medicine) is a General and Child Pyschiatrist and founder of the Matrix Center for Mental Health and Well Being as well as the Premenstrual Syndrome Clinic, both in Pittsburgh, PA. She has been a psychiatric consultant to the NTL Institute of Applied Behavioral Science for more than fifteen years. She also serves as a Physician Advisor for Intracorp Insurance Company where she performs managed care reviews for psychiatric hospitalizations. Dr. Siewers is a member of the American Medical Association, the American Psychiatric Association, and the Regional Council of Child Psychiatry. She has had a special interest in learning and behavior problems in children.

Paul Rodenhauser (Jefferson Medical College) has had administrative and clinical experience in private psychiatric hospitals, although academic pursuits had dominated his career. At Wright State University School of Medicine, Dayton, OH, he served as Director of Residency Education and Chair of the Department of Psychiatry. His previous teaching appointments include Johns Hopkins University School of Medicine and the University of California, San Diego. Clinical, teaching, and research interests include inpatient and outpatient general adult psychiatry, educational strategies, and administrative psychiatry. He is a member of the editoral boards of *Administration and Policy of Mental Health* and the *Journal of Art Therapy*, and a reviewer for *Academic Psychiatry*. Dr. Rodenhauser is Professor of Psychiatry and Director of Medical Student Education in Psychiatry at Tulane University School of Medicine, New Orleans, LA.